INTENTIONAL POSSIBILITY

THE MAGIC OF HAPPINESS AND THE POWER OF CHANGE

Lorna
You bring great
peace and inner healing.
I loved working with you
at TTI?
Big Hug
Sergio Sedas

SERGIO W. SEDAS, PHD

FOREWORD BY JACK CANFIELD

Best Selling Author of The Success Principles™, Dare to Win,
and The Chicken Soup for the Soul® series

Disclaimer

This book is designed to provide information in regard to the subject matter covered. It is sold or provided with the understanding that the publisher, author, editor, and/or sponsor are not engaged in legal, financial, counseling, or other professional services. If legal, financial, counseling, or medical assistance is required, the services of a competent professional should be sought. The publisher, author, editor, and sponsor shall not be held liable in any degree for any loss or injury due to any omission, error, misprinting, or ambiguity.

Edited by Kathryn Marion, www.KathrynMarion.com

Cover design by Renato Urot, Jr., www.RenatoUrot.com

Discounts begin with orders of only 25 copies. Custom orders are also available. Would you like to have Dr. Sedas speak to your group to share the power of *Intentional Possibility*? Visit **www.IntentionalPossibility.com** for more information.

ISBN upon 2016 release: 978-0-9967808-0-3

This is a 2015 Advance Copy

Printed in the United States of America
10 9 8 7 6 5 4 3 2 1

"The fact that you are reading these words means that you are ready to take the next step to intentionally create new possibilities in your life. Congratulations on making the choice to take your life to the next level. Here's my advice: Don't just read this book. Study it. Do the exercises and share what you are learning with your family, friends, and colleagues. Do everything you can to absorb every word in this wonderfully written book. Then put it all in action ... one step at a time. When you finish reading, you will have begun a new chapter in your life. You will be on the path to fulfilling your potential and achieving greatness."

—Jack Canfield

Best-Selling Author of *The Success Principles*™, *Dare to Win*, and *The Chicken Soup for the Soul*® series

To my wife, my partner in love

ACKNOWLEDGEMENTS

I am truly blessed to constantly meet and be surrounded by wonderful, supportive people. Family, friends, and mentors who love me, support me, and inspire me to move forward.

First and foremost, I want to thank my wife, Lory, my mentor and friend, Jack Canfield, my wonderful coach, Jan Fraser, and my editor, Kathryn Marion. You are the support and encouragement that made this dream possible.

In my life, I have met hundreds of people with incredible and inspiring stories, some of which I have written here today. Jesús Teniente, Guillermo Díaz Lankenau, Rosa Ramirez, Adar Villa, María de Gasperín, Javier Prieto, Eder Delgado, Alejandra Zuñiga, Mily López, Ismael Muñoz, and Ricardo Cantú Leal. I thank you for being an example and inspiring me to pursue my dreams.

I want to thank people who have been a great influence in my life: Red Whittaker, Mel Siegel, Rachel Burcin, Caroline Rochon, Romeo Marquez Jr., Mykola Lansky, Puja Gupta, my coaches Jill Cahill, Tiffany Wake Peters, and Sean Smith, and colleagues from the Best Sellers Writers Club: Amy Cady, Jennie Richie, Arnita Jones, Monique Kainth, and Cheri Rainey.

I want to thank Dr. Carlos Mijares for believing in this project and clearing a path that has led to thousands of people discovering their voice and their passion and making a difference in their families, workplaces, and communities.

Finally, I want to thank *you* for joining me in this journey of influence and inspiration. Together we will grow and create a significant and wonderful life full of intentional possibilities.

ABOUT THE AUTHOR

Dr. Sergio William Sedas is an award-winning author and international high-human-potential trainer. He uses intentional possibility to cause positive transformation in life, communities, and organizations.

Funded by NASA, U.S. Air Force, National Science Foundation, and CONACYT, Dr. Sedas received two Master's degrees and a PhD in robotics and computational design from Carnegie Mellon University. There he worked on numerous initiatives including ASE (Automated Simultaneous Engineering) and DANTE, the first robot in history to enter a live volcano in Antarctica.

Upon graduation, he traveled into México in a quest to improve education, manufacturing, and quality of life. He held a number of high management positions at Phillips, Motoman, and Techmatec and also founded companies to develop state-of-the-art robot and vision systems for the automotive industry. He is a well-known author of numerous innovations that resulted in millions of dollars of savings, including the first robot and vision systems to automatically inspect automotive frames in North America.

His passion for education led him to Tecnológico de Monterrey, one of the leading universities in México. He was the Head of the Mechatronics academic program and Director of Strategic Programs where he launched initiatives which would inspire freshman into active learning by engaging in the design and construction of robots that could perform tasks in the real world.

His constant commitment to the betterment of life won him the recognition of Pittsburgh AIDE (Alliance for Innovative Development and Education) for his contribution to robotic technology and education in México.

For over twenty years, Sergio has studied and engaged in possibility and cognitive science to create engagement, intrinsic motivation, creativity, learning, increased self-confidence, and resiliency in students, adults, and organizations. His work in learning through understanding and possibility influenced the design of a national program to develop self-confidence, resilience, and passion in first-year undergraduate students.

He has been a keynote speaker and trainer for corporations, governments, TEDx, universities, and nonprofit organizations seeking to use the power of possibility.

TABLE OF CONTENTS

FOREWORD

Sergio Sedas is a master of intentionally creating possibility. He established himself in a research lab that enabled him to design and build a robot to explore a live volcano. He successfully obtained funding from NASA, the U.S. Air Force, and the National Science Foundation to pay for his schooling. He invented multiple hi-tech companies in México, and positioned himself as a supplier of international Fortune 500 automotive manufacturing companies. He has also created powerful educational programs that have inspired young minds to actively learn how to face and overcome overwhelming challenges.

And ... he invented the possibility of this book.

In my life's work of teaching *The Success Principles* around the world, I have seen hundreds of thousands of people apply those principles in their lives to accelerate their personal, spiritual, and professional growth. Every year, I select 100 professionals from all over the world to train and work with me to learn how to teach these principles and techniques in order to make a significant difference in other people's lives.

Of all the hundreds of people from more than 40 countries I have trained and worked with, Sergio is one of the most outstanding trainers to graduate from this program. Within a very short time, he became a successful international speaker and created numerous programs and initiatives that have influenced the lives of more than 3,000 people. That is truly making possibility happen.

The fact that you are reading these words means that you are ready to take the next step to intentionally create new possibilities in your own life. Congratulations on making the choice to take your life to the next level. Here's my advice: Don't just read this book. Study it. Do the exercises and share what you are learning with your family, friends, and colleagues. Do everything you can to absorb every word in this wonderfully written book. Then put it all in action, one step at a time. When you finish reading, you will have begun a new chapter in your life. You will be on the path to fulfilling your potential and achieving greatness.

Sergio once told me, "It is not that great people make great projects happen. But, rather, that taking on great projects make people great."

I agree.

Here's to your *unlimited* success!

—Jack Canfield

Best Selling Author of *The Success Principles*™, *Dare to Win*, and *The Chicken Soup for the Soul*® series.

INTRODUCTION

*"Many people believe that great people make the extraordinary happen.
I believe the opposite is true; it is doing the extraordinary
that makes people great." —Sergio Sedas*

Here, there, and everywhere ordinary people make extraordinary things happen:

- They start community projects.
- They organize events.
- They form study groups.
- They bring people together.
- They compete in the Olympics.
- They climb the tallest mountains.
- They get better jobs.
- They live incredible relationships.
- They launch wonderful initiatives.
- They start hospitals.
- They design new and exciting products.
- They start parent-teacher projects.
- They start rallies.
- They generate prosperity.
- They inspire people to greatness.

People who do the extraordinary start with an idea—an idea that inspires them, moves them. It may be something they believe is important, like the possibility that "everyone who needs an organ transplant will have one available" or something fun like "our whole class celebrating an academic achievement." As soon as someone has this inspired thought, they create it in possibility by thinking and behaving as if it were already a reality: they communicate it to others; they share it; they think of something concrete to do and act on it; they get other people involved. In short, they begin to *live* it.

Perhaps these people create a campaign to raise awareness and increase organ donations or plan a celebration at the end of the semester. You see, in their minds, this idea is no longer just an *idea*, a longing, or something that *someday* they hope to do.

In their minds, it has turned into *reality*—it *exists*. In their mind's eye, they already have a clear picture of what their project, initiative, or party looks like and how it will play out.

You hear them say, "We are implementing a campaign to raise awareness and increase organ donations" or "We are having a party on Friday night to celebrate the end of the semester." And when they do, these intangible ideas become real.

Not only do the ideas become real in their *own* minds, but in ours as well, and others join in. They start to contribute ideas and actions as they say, "We will hang posters all around school," "We'll contact the radio station and invite a speaker," "We'll organize a fundraiser dinner event."

The more they speak, the more the new idea takes form.

People who do the extraordinary ask for what they want. They invite others. They persist—and thus, they get what they want and need. Then, as more people begin to live their reality, things begin to happen and that which started as a simple idea quickly takes shape.

"We need money for posters," says Hilda.

"I'll contact our local radio station," says Joe.

"Great! I'll ask my friend who is a graphic designer to do the graphics for us," says Mary.

"I'll find out how much printing will cost," says Mike.

As people become engaged, they begin to live in the reality of the possibility that was created. They commit, they take action, and they communicate while enrolling others in this new reality. Soon, there are dozens or even hundreds of people participating: putting up posters, reading the posters, posting on Facebook, or contributing with money. Assisting. Attending. Talking about it.

Many people become engaged in a reality created by a single thought. That is the power of possibility: taking a single, simple idea and bringing it to life. We need to modify our perception so we no longer consider it 'just an idea,' but see it as something real—then act, communicate, and persist until it comes to fruition.

People who do the extraordinary begin this way—with simple ideas. Then, by living in the possibility that they created and sharing it with others, their ideas take on a life of their own. Soon, the ideas become reality for many. But their ideas are not just *any* ideas—they are initiatives that come from a passion they have within. They have purpose, and these purposes inspire us to contribute and make a difference in the lives of others.

When we work to inspire, contribute, and make a difference in the lives of others we become significant: we become leaders; we become mentors; we become friends. It is at the moment in which we are completely engaged in this quest for life that we truly live the ecstasy of life: we are engaged; we are driven; we are inspired; we live with purpose. And we intentionally pursue great challenge with enjoyment and incredible persistence.

MY EXPERIENCE WITH POSSIBILITY

My first encounter with possibility was in 1991. It was then that I experienced the full power of being able to create—and enlist others in pursuing—a new possibility, and how taking action in the space of this new possibility can make it real.

I was a graduate student at Carnegie Mellon University working on my dissertation. At the time, I was about a year from graduation and was unsure of the path I would take. My advisor, William 'Red' Whittaker, and I were participating in a powerful human potential seminar. The seminar promised to help me identify who I was and establish a direction for my life and career.

My classmates and I were all engaged in finding out "who we were" when my advisor stood up and, out of the blue, declared that within a year we would design and build a robot that would enter a live volcano in Antarctica. Before that moment, he had only an idea. But upon making that declaration, he created the possibility of the first robot in history to enter a live volcano.

He began to speak this possibility to students, faculty, NASA, and sponsors. He attracted funding and a team, all of which became a part of that possibility. Within a year, we raised over two million dollars, convinced other universities and organizations to participate, teamed up with NASA, and designed and built DANTE, the first robot in history to enter a live volcano!

Many years have gone by, yet I clearly remember when he stood up in front of us and made that declaration. All of us were novices—the experts were busy on other projects. However, when he asked for someone to lead the development of a vision-sensing system, and looked straight into my eyes, I knew that I had to raise my hand and take on the challenge. He had enlisted me, not only in the possibility of us designing and building this robot, but in the possibility of leading part of the team that could get this done.

It was then that I realized the power of intentional possibility.

By simply making an inspired, powerful, and intentional declaration and constantly sharing it as if it already is, you can create a mind shift that inspires people and organizations and brings them onboard. Once they are enrolled, people move and communicate to make the possibility real.

Wow! Just think of it:

You can stand up and declare something that moves you and then, by engaging people with that possibility, you can get them to give you the funds, resources, and time to make it happen.

I have since used intentional possibility to: create the first hi-tech companies of their kind in México; create inspiring, international educational programs for over a thousand students; launch community benefit programs that inspire young minds and sponsor nonprofit organizations; become an award-winning author and international speaker influencing the lives of tens of thousands of people;

and invent my own position at the university, which enables me to continue to do what I love best: bringing out the best in people and helping them be and do the extraordinary.

Looking back at all of this, I admit it: I live a wonderful, significant, and prosperous life. And you know what? *So can you*!

WHY DID I WRITE THIS BOOK?

I wrote this book for one simple reason: I believe you are ready. You have a powerful voice inside of you that is a source of incredible inspiration. By learning how to release it, you will make amazing things happen. You will enhance and enrich the lives of people around you and, in the process, you will create an amazing, significant, and prosperous life for yourself.

I have worked with thousands of people who have used the methods outlined in this book to start companies and projects that are improving the lives of tens of thousands of people. In the process, they became strong voices in their communities and attracted leaders and people of influence. All of them have made incredible possibilities happen.

If you want to learn to intentionally create possibility, just think about this: unless you are constantly living in possibility, sooner or later, even with all of your current accomplishments and successes, you will feel stuck. And when you do, you will fall into the trap of complacency. Not because you are unable to dream, but because you forgot what to do with your dreams.

With possibility, you can awaken your passion and make the extraordinary come true. You deserve to be happy and live an extraordinary life. You have what it takes to make a difference. All you need is a space for reflection and the right words to guide you along your way.

Everyone can create possibility

Is everyone able to intentionally create possibility? The short answer is *Yes!*

Once you know how, it's as simple as throwing a switch.

In this book, I will teach you how to throw the switch and open the gate that will bring intentional possibility into your life and the lives of others. You will learn the theory and apply it through exercises and projects which will help you experience incredible possibility in your life.

THE STRUCTURE OF THIS BOOK

This book is divided into two major parts:

Understanding Possibility: The first part of the book helps you understand what possibility is and what forms it can take to create positive change on a small or large scale.

Creating Possibility: The second part helps you begin to think about possibility in your own life and outlines the steps to make it a reality.

HOW TO MAKE THE MOST OUT OF THIS EXPERIENCE

It is important that you both *understand* and *feel* possibility and then intentionally *create* possibility. The concepts are simple, yet until you become aware of possibility, they may seem a bit abstract. How do you know you've got it? It will hit you. You will know you do when you do.

I recommend that you:

Keep a notebook with you so you can write out your ideas and reflections.

Read these chapters over and over again. Consult with the book as often as you like.

Do all of the exercises. They are designed to help you build up possibility. More exercises, outlined in detail, to help you practice and perfect your unique style of creating possibility in your life and your community as well as additional information and resources can be found at **www.IntentionalPossibility.com**. Bookmark the site because more valuable resources will be added in the future.

When you live your project, concentrate on the steps, not the outcome. You will achieve positive transformation through the process. The outcome will come, and what you learn will continue. Simply open your heart and allow the amazing person who is already inside of you to come out. You have a lot to give to yourself and those around you.

MY PROMISE TO YOU

My promise to you is that, by playing the game full-out, you will:

- learn to live your life with intent and purpose;
- learn to awaken what is already inside of you;
- feel alive and vibrant;
- learn to create projects, express yourself fully, and inspire and lead others;
- learn to be comfortable asking for what you need;
- learn to make amazing things happen; and
- learn how to create a prosperous and amazing life for yourself and others.

I promise that you will create a wonderful, significant, and prosperous life. And, in so doing, you will positively impact your community, maybe even the world.

UNDERSTANDING POSSIBILITY

WHAT IS IT?

WHAT DOES IT LOOK LIKE?

WHERE CAN POSSIBILITY BE APPLIED?

INTENTIONAL POSSIBILITY

We choose to go to the moon. We choose to go to the moon in this decade and do the other things, not because they are easy, but because they are hard, because that goal will serve to organize and measure the best of our energies and skills, because that challenge is one that we are willing to accept, one we are unwilling to postpone, and one which we intend to win, and the others, too.
— John F. Kennedy, Rice University Stadium, September 12, 1962

A single statement given by John F. Kennedy in 1962 resulted in millions of dollars and thousands of people uniting to place the first man on the moon. People all over the world watched this historical moment on TV.

Putting a man on the moon is a feat worth remembering. But perhaps more important is the fact that all of this occurred because of a single statement. Prior to John F. Kennedy declaring to himself and to the world the possibility of a man on the moon, the idea simply did not exist. People did not talk about it. Scientists did not concern themselves with it. Congress did not invest in it.

It was only when John F. Kennedy declared the possibility of landing a man on the moon—and publicly declared it—that the magic of possibility happened. Once he did, an idea that did not previously exist suddenly became real. It became real not only in his mind, but in the minds of millions of people around the world.

You and I have that same power. We have the power to invent and declare possibility. And, by doing so, we can cause amazing things to happen and intentionally create an amazing, significant, and prosperous life for ourselves.

WHERE IS POSSIBILITY?

Possibility is everywhere. It is there when you are inspired; when you are moved to take action; when you actively pursue a goal; when you create; even when you declare a vacation. It is a state of mind. As such, it governs your thoughts, your actions, and your behavior. It starts with a simple idea. You jump into it. You live it. You continuously think about it. You repeatedly talk to people about it. You take it with you everywhere you go. It becomes your reality. It becomes your life.

Inspired by this possibility, new ideas pop into your head. You create events, products, projects, and initiatives. You take action. People you share it with take action. And, soon, ideas and concepts born in possibility begin to sprout: a concert, a building, a museum, a party, a company, a new job. Each one is a manifestation of the possibility you created.

Possibility quickly becomes viral. When you share possibility with people, you infect them with the new possibility. They take it with them, and it becomes their reality. Inspired by this possibility, new ideas pop into *their* heads. *They* create events, products, projects, and initiatives. They take action.

When you share possibility with others, they share it, more people take action, and pretty soon *those* people have even more ideas and concepts, and give life to their own creations. Each of these is a manifestation of the possibility *you* once created.

Possibility takes on a life of its own. As people live in possibility, they contribute their own ideas and start their own projects, events, and initiatives. The possibility that you created begins to manifest itself in many different ways— some work, some don't; some meet expectations, some exceed them; but all are part of the process that makes possibility grow and expand.

WHAT DOES POSSIBILITY LOOK LIKE?

Possibility takes on many different forms. It will be different for each of you. To help you see what kinds of things can happen in possibility, here are the stories of several successful initiatives … there are hundreds more and, one day, *yours* will be among them.

*   *   *

POSSIBILITY: OHANA

One weekend afternoon, two girls are walking down the street in their neighborhood, when they suddenly spot a homeless child. He is dirty, tired, and hungry.

They begin to wonder what it would be like to give this child, and so many others like him, an experience of love. So they imagine creating a summer camp for state home orphans, hosted by all of their friends. In their mind, their idea begins to take shape as they visualize the kids playing, their friends leading activities, and the smiles on each of the children's faces.

They are completely immersed in their thoughts and can actually envision themselves right there. They see people talking with kids and imagine the conversations that are taking place.

Their bodies respond. Their breathing speeds up with excitement. They feel the joy around them.

Excited, they soon begin to talk with their friends. In their friends' minds, each one of them is participating in the event. They, too, become fully engaged as they begin to offer ideas and suggestions.

"Let's have it at school."

"Mike and I will organize a fundraiser."

"I can get the food."

Somebody's eyes illuminate, and, with a wide smile on their lips, shrieks, "Why not have it be a sleepover?"

"Yes," says another. "We can have them sleep on the gym floor."

"Or," one chips in, "we could get some tents and have a sleep-out."

"Yes, let's have some activities. I'm sure they would like it."

Everyone is fully engaged. In their minds, they are living the experience of this summer camp, complete with thoughts, feelings, conversations, and emotions. Still engaged and immersed in this possibility, they speak with their peers, teachers, and sponsors.

These people also feel drawn to the idea of creating a summer camp, and begin to experience it as if it were already real. They become active participants in making this possibility real: one of them speaks to the dean; two organize a fundraiser; three of them go to speak to a state home.

Everyone is living the possibility as if it were real. They live in anticipation of the excitement, joy, and passion for what they are about to do. You see, in their minds and imagination, this project is alive. They have just created possibility.

This is a true story. In two short years, OHANA—a project created by two high school girls in the city of Monterrey, México —grew to include more than 100 volunteers. Every year, students, faculty, and school administrators organize a one-week summer experience for children of the state. Companies and organizations sponsor the event.

The project has taken on a life of its own. The founders have since graduated from college, and the project continues with a well-defined student leadership council. It has inspired students from many high schools and college campuses who have chosen to immerse themselves in this possibility and replicate it in their own communities.

*   *   *

POSSIBILITY: NOLIMITS

In 2008, I was inspired by the possibility of an environment in which teenagers increase self-confidence and learn by intentionally engaging in challenging projects. I had recently been appointed head of the Mechatronics Academic Program at my university, and I noticed that students near graduation were just starting to get involved in projects. They did not participate in international contests, and they lacked advanced skills which could boost their professional careers.

Inspired by this possibility, I set out to create a program that would engage students in active learning and building complex mechatronics systems. I started by speaking to a class of thirty students about learning to learn by doing and I laid out a challenge of literally putting on the gloves and intellectually competing with MIT. Just as many Olympic athletes do, I knew we needed to start when they were young, so we engaged students as soon as they started the Mechatronics program.

A few days later, a group of ten students and I started this first graduating class of NOLIMITS: Eduardo, Erik Pizaña, Marian Colorado, Aristh Valdiviezo, Abel Trejo, Luis Brunswick, Joaquin Mascareñas, Samuel, Xochitl, and Erick Pizaña. We met every weekend and all of them lived the dream and created their projects.

Since our goal was to create high-performance teams to compete against MIT, we had to do things differently: we needed to accelerate learning and enhance understanding. This meant we needed to change the way I taught and the way they learned.

In four months, I wanted students to learn the specific knowledge, skills, and understanding that are normally spread out over a five-year program. I wanted them to be inspired to engage in their own after-school study sessions and activities. And I wanted them to accelerate their learning and understanding by engaging in hands-on activities which would allow them to build, test, and learn by doing.

More than a course, more than an event, more than a group of people, NOLIMITS became possibility. It was the possibility of students working in industry and in research centers to design industrial robots, medical devices, prosthetic devices, systems to improve farming and cropping, systems to save energy and provide better home environments, innovations in automobile transmissions, devices to improve quality of life by overcoming physical disabilities ... you name it. It was the possibility of these students advancing their studies and their contributions. And yes, it was the possibility of students putting on their gloves and pitting their wits against MIT.

NOLIMITS had life.

Twenty-three students were enrolled in that first class. Led by one, the group began to give NOLIMITS shape. Inspired by the idea of creating a high-performance team, the team designed a curriculum backed up by MIT's Open Courseware.

Using context-based learning, we ensured that, at the end of each class, students had designed and built something. Over a period of 15 weeks, the students attended sessions on Saturday afternoons to minimize conflicts with other extracurricular and sports activities. Each was three hours long to allow time to learn a new theory and implement the resulting projects. And at the end of the semester, every team was required to design their own project.

It was cool! I was so excited and inspired when, at the end of the semester, these teams had built some amazing things. They built electronic games and devices that were showcased center stage at a show-and-tell event organized by seniors. Everyone was impressed by their projects, but, more importantly, the audience was impressed by their youth and energy.

NOLIMITS is alive.

The first graduating class of NOLIMITS became the first instructors. They studied and worked over Christmas holidays and returned to campus with a syllabus, a list of activities, and a kit of components to teach first-semester students.

As more students began to graduate from this program, the question that prevailed was "What now?" Following the philosophy of context-based learning, we encouraged them to volunteer in industry, academia, and research centers, to compete in contests, and to join entrepreneurial programs.

A group of students approached Reiss Robotics, a leading robotic company expanding their operations in México. They were invited to participate in the installation of a manufacturing line over the summer. Over the course of two months they installed, connected, and programmed the machines and robots.

Another group decided to take a leadership role on the MINI BAJA project, an ongoing student group that designs and competes with BAJA-type motor vehicles.

Another group joined a research team led by Dr. Jorge Cortez, where they began to design a prosthetic arm, developing the electronic connections and controls to move it on muscular impulses.

The NOLIMITS possibility was alive and manifesting itself in full force. In just five years, the NOLIMITS program expanded tremendously:

Over 1,000 students have graduated from the program. Inspired by NOLIMITS, graduates and instructors created the Robotics and Mechatronics Club as well as NOLIMITS II, an advanced program for NOLIMITS graduates which brings them in contact with advanced topics and greater challenges.

NOLIMITS also has reached beyond our University. In 2009, NOLIMITS was adopted by Johns Hopkins University for its Center for Talented Youth (CTY) summer program at Tecnológico de Monterrey.

Multiple high schools in Monterrey adopted NOLIMITS as their training for advanced placement certification in Robotics. The year he became coordinator, Ricardo Hernández replicated NOLIMITS at the University of Tabasco, his hometown.

Adar Villa, a student of the Mechatronics program, along with a group of his friends decided to take this further. They contacted governors from several different states and launched an initiative that would build upon NOLIMITS to inspire hundreds of high school students all around the country.

His first summer, Adar and nine volunteers set out to tour the country offering their program to over 300 underprivileged kids in five different states. It was moving to see how the parents experienced hope and immense pride when they saw their children were able to design and build robots. This experience forever changed their lives as well as the futures of those children and families.

What happened to the graduates of NOLIMITS? There are too many success stories to tell, but here are a selected few:

Soon after running his campaign, Adar Villa, while still an undergraduate student, incorporated a company that would inspire high school students through mechatronics. In less than a year, it grew to over nine offices in México and South America. For his successes, Adar received the Young Entrepreneur of the Year award from *Expansión*, a prestigious business publication.

During his second academic year, Guillermo Díaz Lankenau was invited by NASA to lead the design and development of GROVER, an autonomous robot designed to explore ice caps in Greenland. This led him to Alaska, where he presented the project in front of NASA officials; to Carnegie Mellon University, where he participated in their Summer Scholar Program; to a prestigious university in Korea where he advanced his undergraduate studies; then to John Deere where he started an initiative to do applied research and development in México ; and finally to MIT.

During his second school year, Rodrigo Llarena, a graduate and instructor of NOLIMITS, designed, built, and sold his first machine for the coffee industry in Guatemala.

After participating in advanced activities during most of his undergraduate program, Luis Brunswick developed an advanced computer vision system to inspect metal aerospace parts. This undergraduate course project won him an invitation to work at a leading aerospace manufacturing company.

Every day I find what I believe are traces of NOLIMITS. I will never know if those ideas began as seeds of inspiration from our program, but what I do know is that the possibility we created has made the world a better place.

*   *   *

POSSIBILITY: IMPROVING QUALITY OF LIFE

It was a Wednesday morning when Alejandra Zuñiga entered my office. She introduced herself as a teacher for special education. She wanted to talk to me about Francisco. Francisco is a wonderful and smart ten-year-old boy. He has an incredible smile and quickly warms the heart of everyone who meets him. He also has cerebral palsy.

Because of his illness, Francisco cannot use a computer—he cannot control his arms or fingers and, therefore, he cannot use a keyboard. Furthermore, his speech is slow and scattered, so he cannot use voice recognition software.

So, without a keyboard, Francisco cannot use a computer. This means that he cannot use Google, Microsoft Word, Excel, PowerPoint, Facebook, or any of those tools you and I take for granted. Because of this, he would fall behind in his studies and find it very difficult to ever enter college.

Alejandra was in my office to see if we could build Francisco a special keyboard with an Enter key and four large arrows with which he could control the movement of the mouse and cursor. Although this can be done easily, it would be difficult for Francisco to control, so we set out to create something better.

Inspired by Francisco, Mily Lopez, an undergraduate student at the time, took it upon herself to design an interface that would enable him to use the computer. Fully engaged in this project, she interviewed Francisco, his doctors, and his mentor. She also spoke to faculty and students at Tecnológico de Monterrey looking for people who knew about technology.

Finally, after four weeks, she discovered something that made a complete difference: Francisco could control his thumb. That was all she needed to know. She set out to find a "thumb mouse"—a $15 device that can be attached to the hand and controlled with a thumb.

A little time to research and $15 was all it took to give Francisco the possibility of college life! Inspired by the possibility that she had created, the student association raised $2,000 dollars to equip Francisco's wheelchair with a computer so he could work both at home and at school.

This project, and the possibility of helping people in need with technology, drove students and teachers to create "Technology for Everyone," a program that brings students, teachers, and mentors together to develop and donate technology that will assist people with physical and learning disabilities.

* * *

POSSIBILITY: SOCCER FOR EVERYONE

Javier Teniente works at a factory. He is a responsible and committed worker. One day, after listening to one of my tapes, my wife repeatedly asked him, "What do you want?" In an exercise that lasted over five minutes, Javier realized that he loved soccer and that he wanted to be a role model for his kids.

He dug deeper into this conversation and suddenly had an amazing idea. He turned around and openly declared that he would create an afternoon soccer school and league for 8- to 12-year-old kids. He hoped to involve children in this activity to give them self-confidence, inspire them to go to school, and encourage them to do something wonderful with their lives.

Inspired by this possibility, he set out to start a program that would attract young kids around the block.

He asked the school for permission to use the schoolyard after hours.

He asked the city to fix the lights so they could play at night.

He asked my wife, a renowned graphic image designer, to help him design a poster.

He started to share this possibility.

Soon, kids began to sign up. The first week he had eight kids; the next the number jumped to twelve; in the third week, over 24 had shown up to participate in the program.

Parents he had never spoken to volunteered to help.

Soon, the community was involved. And Javier had become significant in their community.

* * *

POSSIBILITY: HEALTH AND PROSPERITY

I met Ismael when he was twenty-three. He is smart and joyful. Yet, like many young men, he was confused about the direction his life should take. He was studying architecture in college and also was involved in real estate...yet he felt something was missing. I agreed to coach him.

I asked him, "What do you want?" Ismael realized that his passion was personal health and fitness. Ismael wanted to see everyone following healthy habits such as exercising and eating healthy foods. He also wanted to prosper. He had been working to pay for school. He wanted to generate prosperity for himself and his family. He declared himself in the possibility of generating prosperity and helping people become healthy. We began to brainstorm ideas that would allow this to happen:

- Create or partner with a gym;
- Start a TV program;
- Start a CD/DVD program;
- Open up a restaurant.

Hundreds of ideas flowed. Each one was better than the previous one.

Through possibility, Ismael created a prosperous business inspiring people back into health.

Twenty-one people attended his first program. And he kept on. A few months later, 150 people had participated. And he kept on, driven by the possibility that he had created. Three years later, his project has grown to three health and wellness centers, an online program and in-company partnerships through which he has helped thousands of people improve their habits and health through proper nutrition, exercise, and positive psychology.

All this came from an idea that started in possibility.

POSSIBILITY CAUSES THINGS TO HAPPEN

When a group of people in a community engages in possibility, great things begin to develop:

- An afterschool program for youngsters
- Wheelchair access in every building
- A night out with friends
- Study hall
- Fundraisers
- Community awareness programs
- Non-profit organizations
- A global conference
- A high school reunion
- A community center
- A mall
- A local swimming pool
- A community daycare
- A 10K Race
- A pot luck dinner.

Each of these examples is a creative instance born from the possibility that you have created.

LANGUAGE DIRECTS THOUGHT

We are driven by language. We use language to assign meaning. We use language to interpret things. And we use language to reason.

Research in cognitive psychology and neuro-linguistic programming has shown that there is great power in language. A simple phrase like "I can't" is sufficient to paralyze your behavior. Opposite phrases like, "I can," "I choose to," or even "I won't" will awaken creativity and trigger positive emotions.

Try this:

On a sheet of paper, I want you to make a list of some of the things that you believe you *cannot* do.

For example:

> I cannot generate $1 million between today and tomorrow.
>
> I cannot throw myself from a bungee jump platform.
>
> I cannot tell my coworker that every time she delivers late it affects my performance.
>
> I cannot stop being angry at my sister.

These are just examples of some things you might feel you cannot do. If you are an incredibly optimistic person or someone who has been trained in positive psychology or in advanced human potential training, you may resist writing down things that you believe you cannot do, but I ask you to do it anyway.

For the next two minutes, I want you to repeat the phrases that you wrote down.

For this example, I would probably state:

> *I cannot generate $1 million between today and tomorrow.*
>
> *I cannot throw myself from a bungee jump platform.*

You can repeat these or any other phrases that come to mind.

Stop.

Now, for the next two minutes, I want you to repeat these phrases again, however, you will substitute the word "can't" with the word "won't."

> *I won't generate $1 million between today and tomorrow.*
>
> *I won't throw myself from a bungee jump platform.*

Stop.

Be aware of how you feel. Was there any change in the way you felt when you were repeating the phrases with "I can't" and with "I won't"?

Now, for the next two minutes, repeat the same phrases, only now substitute "I choose to" for "I won't."

> *I choose to generate $1 million between today and tomorrow.*
>
> *I choose to throw myself from a bungee jump platform.*

Stop.

Was there any difference in how you felt when you were repeating the different sentences? Did you feel a difference between the phrases "I can't," "I won't," and "I choose to"?

People who have taken my seminars report feeling different in each of the three scenarios. Many people feel that the phrase "I can't" is restrictive, limiting. They find that it is difficult to come up with a creative solution; it is as if they had simply given up.

"I won't" and "I choose to" awaken different sensations. Some people say "I won't" and immediately react by thinking, "But, in fact, I do." Others feel that the phrase "I choose to" opens their mind to new and creative solutions. Furthermore, a great weight is lifted off their shoulders as they realize that they are in control—they have a *choice*.

YOU CHANGE YOUR REALITY THROUGH LANGUAGE

You and I can change how our minds interpret events simply by shifting the way we choose to listen to and perceive the world around us—and this is done through language. By stating a new belief and immersing ourselves in this new belief, we can empower ourselves to interpret the world in a completely different way. And then, as if on auto-pilot, our minds begin to filter in meanings that are consistent with this new possibility.

*   *   *

It was August of 2005. A year had gone by since I incorporated Techworks, a new company to manufacture robot systems and process parts for top automotive companies. It was a difficult time. We were growing in projects and suffering the pains of this growth. We worked 24/7. I worked 24/7. I worked around the clock until I fell asleep on a black couch I had in the corner of my office. It had become fairly common for me to work long spells without going home to my family.

One day, after a particularly long working spell in which I literally slept at the office for over a month, I managed to escape to my home in the afternoon. It was two-thirty and I had not had a bite of food. On my way home, I was imagining a wonderful encounter with my family. After what seemed like an eternity, I was finally getting a chance to spend some time with them.

I arrived home and, as soon as I opened the door, I heard an incredibly loud racket. One of my kids was running up and down the stairs, while the other was waving her arms up and down. Through it all, there was a lot of screaming and yelling. My twelve-year-old daughter was arguing that it was her turn to watch the television downstairs. It was three o'clock and she was going to sit down to watch Oprah.

At that time, I did not know much about Oprah and the wonderful things she has done. So all that crossed my mind was, "It's three o'clock and my daughter is fighting for the television. I am tired and overworked. I miss my children and I would like to spend some time with them."

In silence, many thoughts went through my mind. "Is that the best use of her time?" "If she has that much free time, couldn't she use it to do homework?" or better yet, "Couldn't she offer to help me at the office? I am sure she could help me answer the phones or type some of my reports," or at the very least, "Why doesn't she get up and join me for lunch? She has not seen me in such a long time."

Needless to say, I felt hurt and I felt insignificant. But because I love her and it had been a while since I had last seen her, I chose not to say anything.

A couple of months went by and I decided to participate in a human potential seminar (something along the lines of what I now teach). In this seminar, they told me that reality is a perception, guided by our thoughts. And—this is the interesting part—that you and I have the power to change our reality simply by shifting the way we choose to listen to and perceive the world around us. The idea that I could change reality simply by changing what I thought about reality seemed farfetched to me, but I decided to give it a try.

So I called home—yet, before I did, I repeated the thought that "My family is extraordinary and each of my children is extraordinary." My daughter, Ana Cristina, answered the phone. After the usual greetings and exchange of love messages, I got into the topic of that previous afternoon. I opened up and *expressed how I felt. How I had been concerned about the use of her time And how I was a little bit hurt, thinking that if she had so much free time she could offer to meet me at the office and help out.*

[Remember that my thought was that "My daughter is extraordinary."]

I listened.

I was very surprised and moved by her response. "Dad, you know that I am very actively involved in community service and community action. Over the past two years, I have visited many communities in México and I can tell you that there is a lot of poverty and lacking. Oprah is helping the people of New Orleans by attracting the attention of people who can give time and money to rescue them from the flood.

It is important that I watch Oprah every day at three o'clock to find a way in which I can get her to México to observe what's happening so she can help us attract the attention we need to help these people."

It was at that moment I realized that my daughter truly is extraordinary.

By creating the possibility that my daughter is extraordinary and by living inside of that possibility, I was able to listen into a different reality, one that allowed me to see how extraordinary she is.

So when I called my daughter, I lived in the possibility of her being extraordinary—and by doing so, I was able to listen to cues that confirm the fact. I began to ask myself, if we are able to create possibility in a conversation, couldn't we create possibility in other aspects of our lives?

Couldn't we invent ourselves as an author, an excellent parent, an excellent employee, an entrepreneur, or an extraordinary friend? Couldn't we take this further and invent the possibility of creating a movie theater, a community center, or programs which help people?

I have found the answer to be 'Yes!'

YOU CAN INVENT YOUR OWN POSSIBILITY

We are able to invent ourselves to be anyone we choose. We are also able to declare in possibility things like theaters, restaurants, programs that help people, businesses, and community projects. By doing so, whether it be to invent ourselves as someone we choose to be or we invent the possibility of something tangible or intangible, we can enroll ourselves to live in this possibility.

By having a conversation with others, you enroll them to live this possibility with you. By collectively acting on this possibility, amazing things begin to happen. People and resources begin to crystallize before your eyes. And that is when things come to life.

In other words, *you have the power to invent possibility and to create a reality so powerful that people move in the direction of making things happen.*

Your mind is an incredible organ. Yet for as complex as it is, research has found that it is unable to discern fantasy from reality. Furthermore, it is you—not your mind—that creates meaning. This can work in your favor as you can declare a meaning and a purpose that empowers you, drives you, makes you feel happy.

Once you declare possibility and allow yourself to live in this possibility, your mind takes care of the rest. It generates feelings, ideas, and actions that are consistent with this possibility. Almost immediately, the possibility that you have created becomes your new "reality." Anything that fits into this possibility becomes a validation of its existence.

For example, if you declare, "I live in prosperity" and you jump into this possibility, you become aware of things that are consistent with this possibility. You begin to appreciate little things in life. You buy coffee in the morning without a conscious debate about whether you are poor or wealthy enough to afford it. You plan your next trip. You monitor your savings. And you invent new business ventures.

If, by chance, you happen to be out of money to buy something, you do not give any more meaning to it than "I don't have any cash right now." It simply means that you do not have money *at this time* and it ceases to be a permanent state.

People who do not live in the possibility of *living in prosperity* feel restricted. They feel that they do not have a choice. When they find themselves without money to buy something, they give it meaning, as if it were a validation that "not having money" is their lot in life. They feel powerless.

In contrast, when you are in the possibility of *living in prosperity* and you find yourself without money, you clearly see that you have a choice. You can choose to leave without purchasing the coffee. You can choose to have someone buy it for you. Or, you can choose to sign an IOU.

You are free and open to the alternatives that living in possibility create. When you are in possibility, everything that is not consistent with the possibility becomes a fact without meaning, which frees you up to be happy, creative, and free.

POWERFUL DECLARATIONS MOVE YOU AND OTHERS

When you declare a possibility which moves you, and you jump into that possibility, you feel engaged, inspired, challenged, motivated, driven, and alive. You unconsciously begin to take action. You feel empowered. You communicate. You generate ideas. And you make things happen.

When you declare a possibility that moves others, you inspire. People you interact with become part of the possibility. If it is their calling as well, they will jump into the possibility. When they do, *they* feel engaged, inspired, challenged, motivated, driven, and alive. They will unconsciously begin to take action, feel empowered, communicate, generate ideas ... and make even *more* things happen.

So, by declaring a powerful possibility, communicating it, engaging others, and living in the possibility, you cause things to happen. You become significant and a powerful voice in your community and a source for positive change.

REALITY IS PERCEPTION

Reality is a perception that is guided by your thoughts.
You can shift your reality by simply shifting your perception.

Reality is a perception that is guided by your thoughts. The beauty of this fact is that you can shift your reality by simply shifting your perception. You can change the way you feel. You can change the way you think. And you can change the way you perceive everyone and everything that surrounds you by simply shifting your perception.

Imagine the following scenarios:

> *You forgot to put the scissors back in the drawer. When you get home your spouse is not happy.*

> *You ask your office mate for a report to be delivered at 3 PM; he brings it in at 4 PM and looks upset.*

> *You have a great idea to build a new recreation center for kids to go to after school. You ask your boss for $100,000 and he says 'no.'*

How do you react?

These are common, everyday occurrences. Although you may believe that there is only one way to interpret them and react, you might be surprised to know that, in fact, there are *many* ways. How you react depends on the meaning you give to each of them at the time.

Next, we will take a look at some case studies so you can see how, in real life, perception truly is reality and how changing our perception can change our reactions, our reality, even our relationships with others.

CASE 1: CHARLIE

Charlie forgot to put the scissors back in the drawer. When he got home his spouse was not happy.

Scenario 1

Charlie drives home and when he arrives, his wife is not happy. He begins to give meaning to this fact.

> *"What did I do this time?"*
>
> *"She's been upset all week."*
>
> *"She is still upset because I did not put the scissors away?"*
>
> *"Why doesn't she understand that I have to go to work?"*

Consistent with these thoughts, Charlie proceeds to have an argument with his wife.

Scenario 2

Charlie drives home. Along the way, he is thinking how much he loves his wife and how much she loves him. He remembers that they both had an incredibly romantic time in Cancun last year.

When he arrives, he notices his wife is not happy about something. He is immediately concerned about her.

> *"Something must have upset her."*
>
> *"What can I do to help?"* he asks.
>
> *"I need the scissors, and you forgot to put them back,"* she says.
>
> *"Oh, you're right. How forgetful of me. Let me get those for you."*
>
> *"I'm sorry. I keep forgetting to put them back. I hope that it didn't cause you too much trouble."*
>
> *"How can I make it up to you?"*

So Charlie gets the scissors and returns them to her. With a big smile on his face, he gets close to her and gives her a kiss. As he does so, he repeats the words, *"I'm sorry. I love you."*

In essence, both scenarios are the same. Charlie forgot to put the scissors back into the drawer and his wife was looking for them. However, the outcome was completely different.

The outcome of each encounter was a result of what Charlie was thinking and believing even before he arrived on the scene. He brought his context with him. His thoughts and beliefs at that time defined the context under which he gave meaning to what happened—and then he simply reacted to this meaning.

What if Charlie could intentionally change his context? In *possibility*, he can.

CASE 2: LINDA

Linda is at work. She asks her office mate, Marge, to generate a report which she needs by 3 PM. It is now 3 PM and the report is not there. Marge arrives at 4 PM and delivers the report. She clearly looks upset.

Scenario 1

Linda believes that her office mate is irresponsible, a slacker, and is always upset. She is sure that Marge is jealous of her because she was recently promoted. So she begins to reason,

> *"Marge is jealous about my promotion. Why can't she simply put that aside and give me what I need when I need it? I am going to have to speak to my boss about her attitude and if I can't do anything about it, I'll simply ask for a transfer."*

Scenario 2

Linda believes that she is in a great working environment. Marge, her office mate, is so sweet, although at times she seems stressed out.

> *So when Marge is late, she begins to think, "I wonder what kept her? Is she okay? I notice she looks stressed out lately." Later, Linda goes to see Marge*

and asks, *"You look a little stressed out lately, and today you were late with your report. I am concerned for you. Is there anything I can do to help?"*

Through her thoughts, Linda brought in a context under which she interpreted what happened. When she believed *Marge is irresponsible*, she created a context under which she gave meaning to Marge's tardiness. The meaning she gave to it, and not the fact that Margie was late, unconsciously made her upset.

In contrast, when Linda believed *Marge is a caring and responsible person*, she created a context in which the only reason why Marge would have been late was because something was wrong. And, unconsciously, Linda responded in a loving and caring manner.

What if Linda could, at any time, intentionally change her context? In *possibility*, she can.

CASE 3: JOHNNY

Johnny has a great idea: to start a community center where kids can play and study together after school. This will create a safe and nurturing environment that will keep kids off the street.

Scenario 1

Johnny believes that none of his ideas is appreciated.

He goes up to his boss and asks for $100,000 to start this project.

His boss says, "It's a great idea, but I can't give you the money."

Johnny thinks, "It is not the first time he turned me down. I can see that I'm really not appreciated in this company. I see them investing in other ideas. In fact, they just gave Nancy $100,000 for her idea. I think I should start looking for another job. It is clear that I'm not appreciated around here."

Scenario 2

Johnny believes that this company is a great place to work. They're very committed to the environment and they really appreciate his contributions.

He goes up to his boss and asks for $100,000 to start this project.

His boss says, "It's a great idea, but I can't give you the money."

Without giving any further meaning to the reply he asks, "Hmmm, I understand. However, it's a great project and I would love to make it happen. Do you have any suggestions about what I can do or who I could approach to get the needed funds?"

Enrolled in the possibility of creating a safe and nurturing environment, his boss replies, "Have you spoken to Linda? She runs the company's recreation center. She might be able to suggest how you can do it.

"You may also want to talk to Frank. Frank is involved with many community projects and is good at fundraising. And if this doesn't work, why don't you try to set up a meeting with the governor. I'm sure that if we team up together, the state and our company could make this happen."

As before, Johnny created a context under which he interpreted what happened. One context unconsciously made him feel bad and react accordingly. The other one empowered him and led him to open up new possibilities.

What if Johnny could, at any time, intentionally change his context? In *possibility*, he can.

BELIEFS AND MEANING

Above were three cases—each had two possible scenarios. The scenarios were the same, but the outcomes were different. What changed?

The outcome of every event and encounter is driven by the decisions you make. These are influenced by what you believe to be true at the time of the incident and the meaning you choose to give things.

When Charlie believed that his wife did not understand him, he interpreted her remarks as consistent nagging. In contrast, when he believed that he was living a wonderfully loving relationship, he was sincerely concerned for his wife.

Likewise, when Linda believed that her officemate was jealous, she interpreted Marge's delay and reaction as spite. In contrast, when she believed that she worked in a company that had a great working environment, she became concerned about Marge's well-being.

Finally, when Johnny believed that his ideas were not appreciated, he left the office disappointed and upset. In contrast, when he believed that his ideas were appreciated, he simply took the "no" answer at face value and began to explore other possibilities to make his project happen.

How you interpret events and, therefore, how you react to them, is governed entirely by what you believe at the time to be true and the meaning you give to the incident. While one meaning is disempowering and can cause you to be upset, a different, positive meaning can empower you.

You can *choose* a set of beliefs and meanings that empower you and, as a result, lead an amazing life.

THE MAGIC OF INVENTING A NEW REALITY

As human beings, we immediately give meaning to every event. From that meaning, we generate new thoughts ... which generate new feelings as well as even more new thoughts and actions. The meaning we give to each event depends on what we think and believe (our perception at the time). We can create a *new* reality by creating new meaning.

Imagine the following scenario: *There's a new movie coming out today. You have been waiting for over three months for it to be released and it's one you really want to see. You have been standing in line to purchase the tickets since 3 AM behind about 50 other people.*

Finally, it is 10 o'clock and the ticket counter just opened. You still have about 20 minutes to wait. You're almost there.

Finally! You buy six tickets. Six o'clock show. You hold your tickets in your hand, smiling, happy, savoring them. They are one of the greatest accomplishments of your day.

You know there will be a huge line at six o'clock, so you decide to go three hours early. Your partner and friends laugh at you. Who in his right mind gets in line at the movies three hours in advance?

You park your car and, just as you predicted, there are already over 20 people ahead of you. An hour goes by. Two more hours go by. The doors are about to open.

Suddenly, to your left, you see a young man walking past the line towards the door. He turns his head, looks at the line, and continues as if he were oblivious to what's going on. He gets in front of the line, opens the door to the movie theater, and walks inside.

Stop for a moment.

Write down how you feel. What are you thinking?

Did you write it down?

I have asked this question to thousands of people and nine times out of 10, people say that they are upset. "How dare he?" "How rude!" "What gives him the right?" "Where is the manager? I want to complain."

Now imagine you're still in line and this just happened. Five minutes later, you see the man exiting the theater with a woman in his arms. The woman has fainted. She is covered in a blanket, and as he carries her out, he is trying to soothe her. He blurts out instructions. "Call an ambulance!"

What do you think *now*?

Do you have the same feeling? Or did it change?

What made the difference?

There are facts and then there is the *meaning* that we give to these facts. The only facts in this story are:

- you were in line at three o'clock in the morning to purchase your tickets;
- you were finally able to purchase your tickets at 10:30 am;
- you stood in line for about three hours before the show;

- a man walked past the line and entered the movie theater; and
- the same man exited the movie theater with a woman in his arms.

Everything else was your own interpretation and the meaning you gave to the facts. Whatever meaning you gave to the man walking into the movie theater caused you to feel and develop new thoughts. If you thought the man had total disregard for the line, that you were "wronged," or that he should have respected the time that you were waiting, then you would feel upset. If you thought that he worked there, you may not have given him a second thought. If you thought that he was a doctor and that he was rushing in to help someone, you may have been concerned.

Whatever meaning you gave to the facts brought about thoughts … which brought about feelings that brought about new thoughts that awoke new feelings … in a continuous cycle.

Now those same thoughts and feelings moved you into a response. You may have simply gotten upset and complained with your friends. You may have decided to look for the manager and accuse the man, requesting that he be removed from the movie theater. You may have felt so wronged that you decided to simply leave the theater. Or, if you thought that he was somebody who was going to help someone else, you might have offered to help.

Let me repeat this message:

When you are presented with an event, you assign meaning. Meaning sparks your emotions and thoughts. These emotions and thoughts move you into action, which in turn generates new events.

You can alter the meaning (and the resulting thoughts, feelings, and actions) by altering your perspective.

POSSIBILITY CAN CHANGE THE WORLD

What if I told you that you have the power to create the community, workplace, organization, and relationships you want? That you can motivate your neighbors and city officials to transform your community into the ideal place. That you can work with your colleagues and company leaders to create a wonderful, exciting, and nurturing place to work. That you can create an organization that you are truly proud of ... and that you can create amazingly warm, nurturing, and open relationships. Are you interested?

Well, you can!

In a moment I am going to share with you stories of people who have made this happen—and they did it by following the six steps to intentionally create possibility.

But that is not all. Keep on reading, and I will teach you how.

POSSIBILITY CAN HELP YOU IMPROVE YOUR COMMUNITY

By living in possibility, you gain the power to launch initiatives that attract people and resources to create parks, lighting, community centers, swimming pools, volunteer training programs, community reading programs, and even schools. It all starts with a clear statement of possibility.

*   *   *

I met Eder when he was not yet 18 years old. He was leading a group of over 50 volunteers that were visiting resting homes and securing warm clothing for the poor. He had been doing this for a number of years. And he was enjoying it!

I asked him how he started and, in his words, I clearly identified his statements of possibility: that all elderly receive love and care and that every family be warm this winter. These two statements of possibility were the foundations for his programs: *Joven Agente,* where young volunteers get together to give love and care to the elderly, and *Navidemos,* an organization that attracts hundreds of volunteers every year who gather warm clothing and drive it to communities in great need.

* * *

Over 20 years ago, Javier Prieto and a group of parents created a possibility that would lead their children to become active leaders and participants in their community. They started SELIDER, a nonprofit organization that teaches outstanding teenagers leadership values and skills through lectures and work meetings with prominent leaders from industry, academia, and government. Thousands of teenagers that have participated in SELIDER are directly responsible for a large number of volunteer programs that help communities in México.

* * *

One day, my wife and I were driving around when we started to notice large ceramic lions on top of roofs and fences. These lions were painted with different themes and colors—some were golden, others were green with yellow spots, others colored with symbols made of wood and steel.

Intrigued, my wife began to ask about the lions. She found out that Luis Alvarez, a member of the community and some of his friends started to make these lions and give them to children in the community. He asked each child to paint his lion and place it on the roof or someplace that was visible. His goal was to bring the community together and help them prosper by letting people know about the skill sets that were available through painters, tailors, carpenters, welders, bricklayers, car washers, and other people that live within the community.

Over 50 lions were produced, each painted in a different color and placed on rooftops. This raised a lot of curiosity and attracted the attention of a local TV station that did a documentary of the lions and the skill sets available in this community.

Wanting to bring everyone together, Luis and his friends organized a "skill fair" where people in the community met in a celebration full of music, food, activities for the children, laughter, and fun.

An artist and possibility brought a community together into friendship and economic growth.

[*Etnología de una producción artística en el espacio público – El león de Tampiquito como detonador de la transdisciplinariedad a través de cuatro dimensiones de su producción artística*, an essay by Lourdes Ruiz]

* * *

For many years I have volunteered in philanthropic programs Rotary International being one of them. I used to actively participate in a Rotary Club chapter that organized a yearly golf tournament to raise funds which were used to build schools. Every year we would plan the event, work hard to organize it, and sell seats to the tournament. We would look for sponsors and organize great gifts that would attract the best and most committed golf players. Every year after we finished the event and donated the funds to the community, our coffers were empty ... and we had to start all over again.

I noticed that many non-profit organizations work the same way. Volunteers dedicate time and effort to raise funds by attracting sponsors or organizing events that can help them raise the money they need to support and manage their programs. Every year their coffers go empty and they have to start over again.

Furthermore, many of the outstanding volunteers—people who are able to get funds and run these initiatives—find themselves needing to work to support their families, and end up abandoning the project in favor of a job with a steady income. Last but not least, with a growing number of non-profit organizations that ask the same companies for sponsorship, access to money has become tight.

I began to think: *what if we could change all of this.* What if we could create a self-sustaining business model that allowed non-profit organizations to have a steady stream of income and volunteers to get paid for their efforts—all without affecting the budget of the nonprofit?

Within this possibility I created a business model that allows a number of nonprofit organizations to receive a steady stream of income while their volunteers get paid. In this model, when a volunteer gets paid, so does the organization. That gives volunteers the possibility and guilt-free motivation to earn income to greatly benefit their organization. Furthermore, volunteers can grow and strengthen the network by enrolling new nonprofits and new volunteers in a non-competitive collaborative network.

[If you are interested in participating in this model, please contact me at youcanhelp@IntentionalPossibility.com]

*   *   *

I recently led a seminar to teach a group of students how to live Jack Canfield's Success Principles, how to find their purpose in life, and how to create possibility. After a week, 41 students came up with nine incredible initiatives. I share some of them with you here.

Esteban Cerda, Martín Martínez, and Jonathan Saucedo are talented athletes who participate in college sports. They realized that many kids from low-income families look for professional sports as a way to improve their economy. While some of these make it to some form of professional level, their life in sports is limited—and sooner or later they are replaced, leaving them without schooling or the possibility of a professional life. Sensitive to this, they created "Recruiting Talent: from the court to a university degree", an organization that seeks to change this by changing the mindset of growing athletes through motivational conferences and providing them with academic scholarships and opportunities.

Victor Gómez, Linda Soto, Maria Fernanda Molina, and Delio Alanís created BiziTza, an organization that transforms quality of life and longevity in people. Their vision is to transform society by developing apps and innovative technologies that improve health care.

How do you teach kids to recycle? Make it fun! Using games and creative projects, Carlos Bermeo, Rodolfo Galván, and Raúl Meléndez created a program to teach kids in school how to recycle. Piggy Banks, pencil holders, sweepers, garden shovels … all of these are things that can be made with empty water bottles. Recycle and have fun!

Patricio Morelos, Iván Torres, Diana Galván, Laura Santos, Tania Castillo, Sayma Salinas, and Elías Perry study political science. They are aware that people need to become more involved and engaged in issues that affect social and city development. But how do you get people involved? Modeled after two initiatives in Barranquilla and Medellín Colombia, they created "#MdeMetrópoli", a weekly space in which people can gather to talk about the changes that are important to their city. Should roads be improved? What about public transportation? Parks? They got a place downtown where people tended to meet and combined it with the opportunity of having food and drink from local establishments. They brought conferences and speakers to the town and become the seed of good ideas and initiatives that they could share with government officials.

* * *

Now it is your turn.

Look around your community. Look at the people. Look at the families. Now imagine an ideal community, one in which people and families have fun and can prosper. What does it look like? How do people interact? How do people communicate? How do they grow? What inspires them? What moves them?

_____

_____

_____

_____

_____

Declare it in possibility.

NOTES:

POSSIBILITY CAN HELP YOU IMPROVE YOUR ORGANIZATION

Manage people and they will do what you tell them to do,
Inspire them and they will get into action.
Enroll them into possibility and they will change the world.
- *Sergio Sedas, PhD*

How can you define your business? What do you do? Who do you help? How do you help them? What positive value do you bring to the people you serve? To your team? To your suppliers?

A few weeks ago, I walked into a postal station. I asked the clerk, "What do you do?"

"I sort mail," he said.

"What for?"

"To organize it and have it ready for our customers," he replied.

"And then what?"

"When they come in, I give it to them."

"And then what? What do your customers do?" I prodded him further.

"They open up their packages." He seemed puzzled that I was asking so many questions.

"And then what?"

"Well, many leave happy because they received something they were waiting for."

"Ok, so sorting mail and packages allows people to receive their packages and be happy because of it. So, would it be fair to say that you bring happiness to your customers by helping them receive things they want and need?"

"Yes!" His face lit up, like he just discovered something.

"Ok, so now think about your business. What else could you do to bring happiness to your customers by helping them receive things that they want and need?" I continued my inquiry.

"Hmmm, I could have a corkboard on which customers can post things they do not need anymore. I could have a computer on-site, which would allow people to order anything they wanted online to be delivered at our facility. I could have special discounts and programs that would help them save money. I could find out what people buy the most and contact suppliers for a discount. I could open up a store and offer some of these things they need more of. I could deliver their things straight to their homes and save them the trouble of coming to us. I could..." He was beginning to see the possibilities of expanding his services, and likely for the first time.

By changing what he did from the action of sorting mail to the possibility of making people happy by helping them receive the things they want and need, he was able to come up with many creative ideas, projects, and initiatives to make it happen. Furthermore, thinking about the possibility of helping people motivated him.

What statement of possibility can *you* declare that inspires you and your organization to create new programs, initiatives, projects, and ventures?

How can you express what you do so you are inspired, moved, and driven? From this reflection, define a statement of possibility.

_____

_____

_____

_____

_____

_____

Declare it in possibility.

POSSIBILITY CAN HELP YOU IMPROVE YOUR WORKPLACE

Possibility can help you create a working environment that you love and enjoy. It can bring your team together and create long-lasting bonds. It can help them discover a powerful and inspiring meaning in the things you do. And generate the enthusiasm and commitment you need to expand and grow your business.

Emma came to see me one afternoon. We were leisurely talking about different things, when I asked her how she was doing. After hesitating and searching through her relationships, she finally said that something was "not quite right" at work even though they were successfully "hitting their numbers."

I asked, "Do you feel appreciated?"

Emma realized that she and her co-workers did not feel appreciated. So I asked her what things would look like if everyone did feel appreciated.

"It would be wonderful! We would all walk in and complement each other on our work. Help each other out. I don't know, I think I would just love the energy around me," Emma responded.

I talked to her about possibility and how possibility can inspire and move people into a wonderful place. Then I asked her to declare a possibility that would describe her ideal company.

She declared this: "The possibility that everyone in my company feels appreciated."

I told her that she would then create a project that would create that possibility, but first I told her about something I had been working with called The 5 Languages of Appreciation in the Workplace: Empowering Organizations by Encouraging People by Dr. Gary Chapman and Dr. Paul White. I went on to talk to her about how people have different ways to show and receive appreciation, and I told her about some of the exercises we do at my seminars.

At the end of this conversation she said, "I know what to do!"

She met with a few of her close colleagues and got them excited about this possibility. And they started to work on her idea.

The following week, she gathered everyone in the company, gave them each three tokens, and explain, "You have each received three tokens of appreciation. These tokens highlight the wonderful qualities and traits you have and the wonderful things you have done for others and for me. Now you are full of appreciation.

"Every day, you are going to share your tokens—your appreciation—with others. Go to someone, give him or her a token of your appreciation, and tell them something about their character or their personality that you like, or perhaps acknowledge something they did for you or others. Hand all of your tokens all out.

"And from now on, when you receive a token and word of appreciation, receive it, savor it, then go off and share your token and appreciation with someone else. You can appreciate someone you are close to, or perhaps someone you haven't yet met but that you noticed that they did something that is worth appreciating them for.

"Let's start today. Take your tokens and share them with others."

People started to come alive as they began to share and receive their appreciation:

"I appreciate that you are always cheerful. I overheard you talking to the customer. She was really distraught and you quickly made her smile. It was wonderful."

"I appreciate your integrity. It makes me feel comfortable knowing that you will be handling our accounts."

"When I walk into your office, I am always inspired by how organized you keep your desk. I really appreciate you being on our team. I believe you will bring order to chaos."

A few weeks later, Emma came back to my office. She was carrying with her a token of appreciation. "This is for you," she said. "I really appreciate who you are and what you have done for all of us. I love going to work."

* * *

Michael, the CEO of an important company, wanted to take the company to new heights, but was struggling to get the energy going.

"People are doing their jobs well. I cannot complain. However, if we are going to expand, we really need to feel excited and driven. You know, the fire-burning-butterflies-in-our-stomachs-excitedly-challenged kind of feeling. "

"Would you mind if I did a simple exercise with your team?" I asked.

"Go for it."

He got his team together and we started to talk about possibility. I told him the story of Red and Mily and all of the people who created possibility—not as a vision, but as a reality; something exciting they could immerse themselves into. And how possibility is always about creating an ideal world and giving meaning to what you do. Then we did a simple exercise.

I asked them to imagine a perfect world. One in which their company makes a difference. One in which their customers are happy and successful. One in which they feel significant and appreciated and they feel proud to share what they do with their families. One in which they are all united, working in favor of a greater good.

They started to define what possibility looked like. They saw people around the world enjoying their products. They saw themselves understanding the people who used their products. And they saw themselves living and thriving in a fun environment.

Once they gained clarity through possibility, it became quite easy to come up with initiatives and programs to make it happen. Excited, they began to enroll their colleagues, their families, their customers and suppliers, and their community.

I saw Michael a few years later. The company had expanded worldwide. People in the company were excited and working together...and they all felt good!

* * *

Margo wanted to get her team to work together. "We come to work, we do our things. But then all is over. I feel that we should be working together as a team helping each other out. You know —like a pack of wolves—she smiled."

"You can bring them together through possibility." I told her. "People who form strong bonds outside of work tend to carry these bonds to the workplace. And there is nothing that will bring you together better than to fight for something significant that inspires you and moves you."

So we started an experiment: they would declare possibility and work on a project that would improve the lives of many people.

We could have focused on things that would improve the lives of people at work – child care, parent's night out, assistance, youth programs for our children. However, it was near the Xmas holidays so we got Margo's team together and decided to talk about people in need. We talked about older people who did not have relatives visiting them. The homeless and children in different communities who did not have warm clothing. And families that would have to spend the holiday season without a decent holiday meal. Then I invited them to declare the possibility of an ideal world.

They got together and declared the possibility that the homeless and children are warm. They jumped into this possibility and began to brainstorm about a project:

"How about we organize a drive to collect money, warm clothing, and food?"

"Why don't we get our families and the community involved? It will be a great activity this holiday season."

"I will get our kids to help us draw and put up posters."

"Why don't we meet at my house to get this started? Will you bring your spouses?"

"I know a community center we can work with—they know a lot of volunteers who can help us out."

Together they created a drive and raised clothing and food for the homeless and children. Their families and friends participated. On the given day, they all went down to the local community center and handed everything out. In the eyes of every person that received their gift, they saw the significance of what they had done, together.

Possibility brought this team together. The bonds and memories forever changed their relationships at work.

* * *

Now it is your turn.

Think about your ideal workplace. What does it look like? In this ideal workplace, how do people interact? How do they communicate? What inspires them? Can they be creative and share ideas? Do they have time with their family? Does everyone feel significant? Do people contribute to each other? Do people know each other? Do they share moments together? What about your customers and suppliers. How can you and your organization make a difference in their lives?

Each of these questions can lead to a powerful statement of possibility.

_____

_____

_____

_____

_____

_____

_____

_____

_____

_____

Declare it in possibility.

NOTES:

POSSIBILITY CAN EVEN HELP YOU IMPROVE YOUR RELATIONSHIPS

You can invent the *possibility of a wonderful relationship* with the people you love and care for, your family, and your peers and co-workers. Stop for a moment and declare the possibility that *you have an extraordinary relationship with your partner*.

Think about the people you love and care about. What is the relationship that you would LOVE to have? Declare it by simply stating, *"I have an extraordinary relationship with my partner."* Let your mind accept it. Immerse yourself in it. Live in it.

Imagine that you get home and find your partner upset. What meaning do you give this event? If you are living the possibility of *I have a wonderful and extraordinary relationship*, you will most likely attribute her being upset with something related to her, not your relationship—a problem at work, personal worries, etc.

When you attach meaning consistent with the possibility of *I have a wonderful and extraordinary relationship with my partner,* it will not be about you having done something wrong; it will be about something that is troubling *her*. And if, by chance, she is troubled by something you did or forgot to do (like take out the trash or pay the bills), you will address it in the space of *I have a wonderful and extraordinary relationship with my partner.*

Let's say that you did, in fact, forget to pay an important bill.

Someone who is not living the possibility of *I have a wonderful and extraordinary relationship with my partner* might interpret it as a scolding, an accusation, a validation that their relationship is *not* good. Or interpret it as a challenge or add meanings which validate an insult.

In contrast, someone living in the possibility of *I have a wonderful and extraordinary relationship with my partner* will simply take a statement at face value—"I forgot to pay the bills"—and, without giving it more meaning, will humbly apologize and immediately complete the task. For someone who is living in possibility, the comment ceases to have more meaning than what it is. And if, by chance, it does receive more meaning, the meaning will be consistent with possibility.

You can take this a step further: you can invent in possibility the quality of any and every relationship you have.

* * *

Jonathan and Angela are very successful in what they do. One works in technology, the other in corporate image. Both are greatly acknowledged in their work. They are married. They have a family of three kids.

However, as with many couples, they are run by their routines. It has been a long time since Jonathan and Angela have spent quality time together, and their relationship has become stagnant. Wake up early. Feed the kids. Off to school. Off to work. Come home. Feed the kids. Finish work because a report is due tomorrow. Watch some TV, and then off to bed.

Don't get me wrong. They have a wonderful family. They have wonderful jobs. And they are life companions. But they want something more. They want romance, love, and passion in their lives.

Jonathan and Angela learned about possibility—and they invented the possibility of a romantic, loving, and passionate relationship.

Inside of this possibility, they began to generate ideas—or "projects" if you will— they could do which would lead them in this possibility.

Excited, they began to brainstorm. How about "Wednesday night out"? No matter what, you and I will go out on Wednesday evenings. One time to the movies; another to dinner; another to dance.

"Yes," says Jonathan. "I love the idea. And how about we plan two weekend vacations—you like the city and I like nature. So, how about on a weekend in May we go off to a beach, and in November we go off to Vegas? Just the two of us— our little escapade."

"I love it!" says Angela.

"Wait, I have another idea," he says. "Because of my business, I travel a lot. My expenses are paid for. Why don't you and I plan it so you can come with me? We will cover your portion of the expenses so you can join me.

"Once I finish my activities, we can enjoy a romantic dinner and spend time together. During the day, you can treat yourself to a mini-vacation—you and I both know that you deserve it."

"But I have to work," she replies.

"Yes, but you are a freelancer. So, how about I let you know in advance so you can prepare? Or if it works best for you, we can extend our stay over the weekend and you meet me there."

"I am excited!"

Soon, living a romantic, loving, and passionate relationship was their reality. They became completely immersed in this possibility. It became part of their life. They started to send each other messages and to surprise each other with a quick lunch here and there, flowers, a card, a gift, and a loving and encouraging message.

They lived full of romance, love, and passion.

You can do the same.

Think about things that you can do to create this. What can *you* do for them? What can you enroll *them* to do? You can even use possibility to create a wonderful relationship with your children and extended family.

_____

_____

_____

_____

_____

Declare it in possibility.

*   *   *

I grew up very independent. Though I loved my parents and we lived in the same city, I would not visit nor call them for months at a time. I loved them, but my mind was focused on my work and my company, and they were not always on my radar ... until one day I hired a life coach.

One of the things my coach asked me was "what do you want?" So I started to review the different aspects of my life: finance, career, relationship, family, personal growth, and others. And I realized that I loved my parents and wanted to spend time with them.

So I invented *the possibility of a wonderful, close, and loving relationship with my parents*. Within this possibility, I thought about meeting with them every Tuesday for breakfast. So we started to do that.

Week after week, we met for breakfast. We talked; we listened. I shared my dreams; they talked about their life and my sisters. No matter what came up, I blocked out and protected this time—this was *our* time.

Years went by and my parents got older. My mother was strong, but my dad became frail and needed great care. On Saturdays I helped my dad bathe and get dressed and fed him breakfast. The three of us spent all afternoon together at their club. We ate lunch and sat there, relaxed, enjoying the evening sunset. At night I would help him get ready for bed.

I continued this practice until the day he passed away. It was a Saturday.

The day he died, all I could think of was gratitude: gratitude for the day I declared the possibility of a wonderful, close, loving relationship with my parents. Gratitude for all the days we spent together. Gratitude for the time I was able to care for him. Gratitude that I was there at the very end.

*   *   *

Think about your own family. What is the ideal relationship you can have? With your children? With your parents? Jot some notes down right here as you think of your ideal family.

_____

_____

_____

_____

_____

_____

_____

_____

_____

_____

_____

_____

_____

_____

_____

_____

_____

Declare it in possibility.

NOTES:

Q & A ABOUT POSSIBILITY

Over time, people have asked a number of interesting questions about possibility. All of them will be answered when you jump into and engage in a life of intentional possibility. In the meantime, here are answers to some of the questions you might have.

What is possibility?

Possibility is defined as a powerful state of reality that you are in when you declare, and engage in, the realization of an inspired thought.

When you declare something in possibility, your mind accepts it as real, and you begin to act and behave consistent with this new reality. As such, you can invent the possibility of anything you desire: a nurturing and fun environment, easy access to every building, a significant and prosperous life, etc.

Once you jump into this possibility, conversations, ideas, projects, and actions begin to emerge.

Will it move me?

Yes. When you are in possibility, you are engaged, immersed, and driven by the possibility.

Why do you call it "intentional possibility"?

Everyone creates possibility unconsciously.

If you have ever been the first to say something like, "Let's have a party on Friday," and, when Friday comes, have seen everyone having a party, you created that possibility by declaring "the party." You created a mental state in which everyone already lived the reality of "there will be a party on Friday."

By declaring the statement, "Let's have a party on Friday," you caused it to exist in your mind and the minds of the people you spoke to.

The same thing happened when the people you spoke to shared it with other people. In their minds, the party on Friday existed, so much so that people started to prepare for it and buy things for it.

They imagined who was going to attend the party, the conversations they would have, even what they were going to wear. They thought about the location. If they were parents, and they had young children, they thought about who they would call to babysit for them.

So, by declaring a simple statement and sharing it with others, you created possibility. Now imagine doing the same thing, but intentionally declaring things which allow you to create an amazing, significant, and prosperous life.

Have I ever created possibility?

Yes. You have created possibility—any time you had an idea which you dove into and immersed yourself in fully, which has spread around and become part of your and others' reality.

How do I make it intentional?

You make it intentional by diving into and *living* the possibility and enrolling others into it.

Do you need to study to generate possibility?

No. Possibility that transcends comes from deep inside of you.

What does living in possibility feel like?

Possibility is a state of mind where the possibility that you have created simply *is* and you may not even be aware that you are engaged and living in possibility.

However, when you are engaged and living in possibility, you feel inspired. You feel engaged, driven, moved, happy, and energized. You are excited when you talk about it, and you are excited when you do things related to it.

You are creative and you can easily generate different alternatives and solutions.

When you are immersed in possibility, you do not think, you simply act. You may feel butterflies in your stomach about asking for something, but you will go forward and ask.

Living in possibility moves you. Obstacles simply become things that need to be overcome. They cease to have any meaning and therefore release the hold of fear that could paralyze you from moving forward.

Why do I feel engaged?

It is an ability of human beings to immerse themselves so much in an activity that everything else ceases to exist. Mihaly Csikszentmihalyi called it "flow," a state of being in which you are completely immersed; time ceases to exist; you're engaged; you're inspired; you are just creating and doing.

This happens a lot when you are doing something artistic like a painting or when you are trying to solve an interesting, yet challenging, problem. It is also present when you play video games or are in a dramatic scenario where you are challenged by adversity and feel inspired to conquer.

Being in possibility puts you into the flow.

Can I change a city?

Yes! Everything you see around you—the buildings, sewers, roads, stop signs, shopping malls, and parks—were created in possibility. Someone had an idea, immersed themselves in the idea, and shared it with other people. Those people then immersed themselves in the same idea and the possibility began to take shape.

For example, they may have thought about creating an environment or an area where kids could play. As people spoke about it, it began to take shape. It may have resulted in a park near your house. Someone could have imagined a playground which crystallized into a seesaw swaying in a sandbox. Someone else might have imagined a baseball diamond. Someone else might have imagined benches.

Then, each of those instances of the possibility of an environment in which kids can play became a possibility themselves. As people got engaged, they began to participate. Banks gave loans, construction companies submitted bids, the city donated land, and residents began to talk about it and planned activities. All of this was created by someone who had an idea, engaged themselves in the possibility, and began to have conversations.

Why do I want to do this?

You can choose to live your life as you already do, and I am sure that it is already amazing. However, as human beings, we have a basic need to feel excited and surprised, a need to be significant, to be challenged, to grow, to be part of a community, and to contribute.

Intentional possibility that moves you and contributes to those around you provides all of that. It challenges you, creates excitement, and even throws in a few surprises. By generating possibility and engaging others in this possibility, you become significant. By contributing to the lives of others and becoming a voice in the community, you are significant to those people.

By facing and overcoming challenges and adversity, you grow. And by making something that is much bigger than you—created from a space of love and service—you contribute immensely to the lives of others.

How can I create something without time and resources?

Time and resources are relative. We all have the same amount of time and access to many of the same resources. It is how we choose to use that time and how we choose to seek and use the resources which makes the difference.

When you live in possibility, you inspire others to become a part of it. People who are engaged offer time, knowledge, and resources to make the possibility happen. As you will discover, creating possibility is not about you doing each and every task that is required, it is about sharing and inspiring others to become a part of it.

What do I need to make it real?

All you need to do is declare the statement as possibility, live in the possibility, share it with others, and move into action.

Why is possibility a powerful state of mind?

It is simply how human beings are designed. We have thoughts, and thoughts create meaning, which creates action. When you declare and jump into possibility, your mind accepts it as real, and you begin to act and behave consistently with this new reality. Your state of mind creates a brand new reality.

What does possibility do for me?

If you let it, and you live it often, it will allow you to create an amazing, significant, and prosperous life.

How long does the feeling last?

The feeling lasts as long as you are in possibility. When you're in possibility and are completely engaged in action, you feel driven and excited. When an event that you created in possibility is finished, you feel complete, and when you remember it years later, the same feelings of completeness, happiness, and peace emerge again.

Experiences are stored in our minds along with the feelings that we associate with them, so every time you bring up that memory, you bring with it all the feelings and emotions you had at that time. You will continue to have these feelings as long as you are engaged in possibility, and you will relive the experience every time you remember.

What if I am shy?

Simply create the possibility that inspires you, immerse yourself into it, and let it drive you. When you're deeply immersed in possibility, you're not thinking about what people will say, what people think, whether you are shy or not, or whether you have the 'right' abilities. You are simply engaged.

What is the difference between possibility and goals?

Goals themselves may turn into possibility as you declare them and visualize them as complete.

What if I am not good at communicating?

Possibility lives in communication. Now, you do not have to possess powerful public speaking or writing skills, but you do need to be willing to put yourself on the line and go out there to share—because possibility is not about manipulating and convincing people, it is about sharing and inspiring. And when you speak from the space in which you are completely engaged and inspired, you will inspire others as well.

So, trust yourself. Be yourself. Live in possibility and share the space.

Now, if you do wish to learn how to speak in public (which is a very valuable skill to have), you may want to seek your local club of Toastmasters® and/or a local speaking coach. Toastmasters® brings together people who want to learn to communicate and inspire others through speech.

So, if possibility is everywhere, where does possibility not exist?

Possibility lives in the space of love, friendship, hope. This is a space devoid of ego, that Wayne Dyer calls it 'high frequency.' This is where possibility exists.

Possibility does *not* exist in a place that is dominated by ego. It does not exist in a space in which you worry what people will say or think. It does not exist in a space where you focus on how only you can benefit from it, at a heavy cost to others (as well as to yourself in other ways).

It is important you understand that you *can* live in prosperity and be in a high frequency—they are not mutually exclusive. You may seek to be happy and at the same time, be in a high frequency.

I know a lot of people who have raised fortunes and their lives by being generous. That may sound contradictory, but the only way you can generate financial rewards is by finding a way in which you can help and give happiness to many other people.

By making it easy for people to purchase and download their favorite songs, iTunes gives millions of people around the world happiness—and, in the process, they created a very profitable business.

By making it easy for millions of people around the world to find and buy books and other items they want on the Internet, Amazon has put smiles on the faces of millions while at the same time creating a very profitable business.

So any possibility that lives in the space of high frequency is good and will inspire others to come along.

I am driven by goals—how can I live in possibility?

There is nothing wrong about being driven by goals. Goals give you clarity. Goals give you a sense of direction. What you might want to look at is whether the goals drive you and engage you toward something that you're excited about, or are they medicine for something you are lacking.

When you are driven by goals, you may well be living in possibility. If you are driven by goals and feel happy when you accomplish the goals, and that happiness persists, then at the time you were pursuing the goals, you were living in possibility.

If, on the other hand, you're driven by goals and feel empty rather than complete when you're finished, you're driven by something you lack. You may feel you lack certainty and believe that the goal will provide it for you. You may feel insignificant and that insecurity may drive you. You may feel alone and the goal allows you to be surrounded, at least temporarily, by many people.

You may feel stuck and in a rut, and the goal gives you a way to feel like you are growing. And you may also feel that you're not contributing to the world, that you are not making a difference, and are motivated by the thought of completion, not the benefits it can bring to people.

What if I fail?

When you are in possibility, you do not fail if something does not work. The only thing that happens is that particular instance of possibility did not work. You can choose to create something different, persist, or find a different solution.

Say that you are *creating an environment that allows teenagers to grow in a safe and nurturing environment.* You choose to create a swimming pool where teenagers can go after school, and this project is at a halt (at this time).

1. Realize that this project is just an instance of the possibility that you have created and that there are other instances that you could create. You could choose to create street soccer, or a basketball court, or a student-run fundraiser for something in their community.

2. Realize that you can still build the swimming pool in another place, or that you could borrow a swimming pool. Or, you simply postpone your date. You modify your plan.

3. Realize that even if you are unable to build the swimming pool, all that has failed is the plan to build a swimming pool. And that is only an instance of the possibility, not the possibility itself. There are many other things that you can do to bring the possibility to life.

4. Realize that there are no failures. There are simply things that work and things that do not work. The possibility you created is greater than any one instance. Within possibility, all you need to do is pick another "what" or another "how." Change the event, program, building, location, date, or change how you are going to implement the plan.

CREATING POSSIBILITY

CAN I CREATE INTENTIONAL POSSIBILITY?

WHAT RESOURCES DO I NEED?

WHAT STEPS MUST I TAKE?

THE POWER TO CREATE POSSIBILITY

I used to think that only great people did great things. I have since come to realize that the opposite is true: it is the act of engaging with great projects and great ideas that makes people great.

Who can forget Martin Luther King, Jr.'s message of possibility that inspired one of the largest civil rights movements, crumbled segregation, and united a nation previously divided by race?[1]

Or the speech made in 1962 by John F. Kennedy, a former PT-109 commander and President of the United States, that made landing on the moon possible?[2]

How about the possibility to give wholehearted and free service to the poorest of the poor, made real by the Missionaries of Charity, a Roman Catholic congregation founded by Mother Teresa, which in 2012 consisted of over 4,500 sisters and is active in 133 countries?

Or the possibility of "creating a world without poverty" declared by a professor of economics, Muhammad Yanus, who developed the concepts of microcredit and microfinance (loans awarded to entrepreneurs too poor to qualify for traditional bank loans)? In 2006, Professor Yanus was awarded the Nobel Peace Prize "for his efforts through microcredit to create economic and social development from below."

---

[1] Martin Luther King. Full speech
http://www.americanrhetoric.com/speeches/mlkihaveadream.htm

[2] "John F. Kennedy, Rice University Stadium, Sept 12, 1962,
http://er.jsc.nasa.gov/seh/ricetalk.htm

All of these men and women were once ordinary. Yet it is through their messages and the possibilities they created that, in our minds, they are extraordinary. They moved people and countries into possibility.

Just like them, *you* have the power to create possibility, to look inside yourself and declare a message so moving it will inspire others into action, realizing the possibility of the vision you hold. It all starts with a thought, a declaration, and a leap into possibility.

LEAP INTO POSSIBILITY

How would you feel if you were doing something that you were really passionate about and you *knew* that, by doing it, you were greatly enhancing your community, your organization, and the lives of many people around you?

How would you feel if you suddenly found yourself surrounded by people who were so inspired by you and what you were committed to, that they wanted to volunteer their time, their resources, and their money to make it happen?

You are going to learn to inspire people to join you. You are going to feel excited, alive, driven. You are going to ask for what you need and keep moving forward. And you are going to find yourself surrounded by people who appreciate you for who you are and what you stand for. In other words, you are going to immerse yourself into a process that will lead you into one of the most exciting and life-altering experiences of your life.

Many people, companies, and institutions have gone through these steps. And in possibility they have launched initiatives that take their lives and organizations to new heights.

Now it is *your* turn.

Yes. It is your turn to experience the tremendous joy, satisfaction, and personal growth that come with creating and living in possibility.

THE SIX STEPS TO POSSIBILITY

In a nutshell, the six steps to intentionally create possibility are:

1. ***Find your purpose and declare possibility***
   First, you will define a clear and inspiring statement of possibility which you will begin to live, share, and communicate.

2. ***Define a project, event, program, or initiative***
   Next, you will define a project, event, program, or initiative that impacts between 50 and 200 people.

3. ***Engage others***
   You will invite and enlist people into possibility by sharing your possibility and inspiring them to actively engage with your project.

4. ***Lay out a plan***
   With your new team, you will formulate a plan.

5. ***Get into action***
   You and your team will tackle the plan.

6. ***Acknowledge and Celebrate!***
   And, through it all, you will make it a point to acknowledge and celebrate yourself and others every single step of the way.

Follow these steps and you will make possibility happen. And, like many others, you will release the greatness that is already inside you.

You will learn important skills that will improve every aspect of your life. You will learn to face great challenges with joy and overcome them with resiliency, excitement, focus, and determination. And you will learn to welcome and overcome uncertainty, resistance, and fear.

You will become a great leader by learning to listen, acknowledging your team, and celebrating your accomplishments. You will learn to communicate and engage others into possibility. You will learn to plan, focus, and get things done. You will learn to overcome discomfort and ask people for all of the things you want and need including money, resources, time, and help. And at the end of the road, you *will* succeed.

Through it all, I want you to remember one thing: *It is NOT about the project; it is all about YOU experiencing the process.* By engaging and going through the process, you will become more confident and you will come to realize that you have become the great person you need to be to make great and amazing things happen.

Are you ready? The game is on!

The only rule is … **play the game full-out!**

STEP 1:
FIND YOUR PURPOSE &
DECLARE A POSSIBILITY

Passion is the fuel that ignites your success! Having passion for a particular goal—personal or professional—provides the energy and motivation to take the necessary action to achieve that goal.
- 107 Ways to Stick to It, Lee J. Colan

Possibility is born in the declaration of an ideal world—a world that manifests itself through projects, events, programs, and initiatives. For example, the possibility of *prosperity and a bright future through education* might manifest itself in a university or a program for high schools. The possibility of *health and well being for everyone* can manifest itself into a hospital, a fundraiser, or a nonprofit organization. The possibility of *a wonderful and family-like relationship at work* could manifest itself as a company picnic, family night, or a powerful seminar.

It all starts with an inspired statement of possibility. In this section, you will define a statement of possibility. Once you make this statement, you will be in a position to inspire and engage people into specific projects, events, programs, or initiatives that are inspired by this possibility.

*   *   *

It was a Tuesday afternoon in my office. I was excited and about to interview Maria de Gasperin, founder of OHANA, a movement which organizes a life-altering summer experience for orphans.

"How did you come up with the idea to start OHANA?" I asked.

"I was studying in Germany at the time. We had organized a drive to raise funds to buy jackets and clothes for kids in México. We raised a lot of money.

"A friend of mine and I were part of the team that went to deliver the jackets. And, while it was a beautiful gesture, I realized that it all ended in one event. There was no follow-up. There was nothing that transcended beyond this kind gesture.

"This troubled us, so we began to think: how can we permanently change their lives? What could we do that would help them experience an environment that would nurture them, let them see how wonderful they are, raise their hopes, and show them the greatness they have inside?

"That is when we declared the possibility of a summer camp for orphans as a space in which we would give these kids a life-altering experience. We would give them comfort, raise their self-confidence, and at the same time teach them values like love, courage, and determination.

"We laid out a plan, gave it structure, and ventured to build the first summer camp. We have done this for over five years now. We have invited over 100 kids and have more than 100 volunteers who are part of the OHANA family."

*   *   *

YOUR STATEMENT OF POSSIBILITY

Your Statement of Possibility will come from something that moves you. That resonates with you. That drives you.

It may come from something you are inspired by, such as creating an environment that promotes happiness in the workplace, or something that promotes prosperity and well-being, or education, or harmonious relationships, or perhaps a safe neighborhood. It comes from a positive cause or message you resonate with which becomes the seed that inspires you into possibility.

But possibility may also come from something that you are fighting for; something that perhaps is not working well which moves you into creating the possibility to make it happen: equal rights, great health benefits, a warm and caring working environment, etc. are all possibilities that are born from things worth fighting for.

In this section you are going to write your own statement of possibility. To do this, I will walk you through three exercises. In the first exercise, you will approach possibility from the space and image of an ideal world, environment, and community.

In the second exercise, you will approach possibility from the perspective of something that you are fighting to make better. In the third, you will simply write or rewrite your own statement of possibility.

Once you have written your own statement of possibility, you will write a short description that paints the perfect image of the wonderful life we can all have by living in your possibility.

EXERCISE #1: COMING FROM AN IDEAL WORLD

Imagine that you live in an ideal world.

- What does it look like?
- How does it feel?
- What are people doing?
- How do they interact?
- What makes it fun to be there?
- What makes you feel good about it?

Write all this down on as many sheets of paper as you need. Start with some of your initial thoughts here: _____

_____

_____

_____

_____

_____

Now, transport yourself into your ideal work environment.

- What does it look like?
- How does it feel?
- What makes it so special?
- What are people doing?
- What are you doing?
- How do people interact with each other? the boss? customers?
- How do the workers feel?
- How do you feel?
- How do the customers feel?

Write this down.

Now, imagine yourself living in your ideal family relationship.

- What does it look like?
- How does it feel?
- What makes it so special?
- How does everyone interact?
- Do you share things with each other?
- Do you celebrate together?
- How do you support each other?

Write this down.

Read it again. You have just created the image of an ideal world which is a powerful starting point to define a statement of possibility.

Now see what you resonate with and write a single statement that describes, in possibility, the ideal world. Start with:

I see the possibility of: _____

_____

_____

_____

EXERCISE #2: A TURN-AROUND STATEMENT FROM SOMETHING WORTH FIGHTING FOR

Imagining an ideal world is a great place to start to define possibility. However, you can also define possibility by observing things in your surroundings that are simply not working. Perhaps you see something that troubles you at work, at school, in your home, or in your community. Something that you feel passionate about, which you believe can be better and that you would like to change.

From this observation of what is not working, you can construct a turnaround statement of possibility that describes the opposite: an ideal world, workplace, and community where things *do* work.

For example, if you are troubled at work by apathy amongst your co-workers, you could turn this around by wishing *the possibility of an environment where people participate and feel their ideas matter.* If you are a school teacher and are troubled by students who keep falling behind in their studies, you could think of *the possibility where students receive all the academic and tutoring support they need to be successful in school.*

In other words, start by thinking about things you worry about and then imagine the opposite. Imagine a world where the opposite is happening, and within this positive and inspirational setting write your own statement of possibility.

Remember to write your statement of possibility in the space of what you want and not of what is missing.

For instance, if you want to end violence, you may seek to find violent alternatives such as stronger use of force, harsher penalties for delinquents, etc. But you should seek the contrasting view as you define your possibility: come from a space of generating peace, which may lead you to create the possibility of schools, community involvement programs, community centers, a big brother/big sister mentoring program, a "street soccer" league for kids, or a community education and development center for parents.

* * *

Streetfootballworld.org is a non-profit entity that supports a worldwide network of organizations that use football as a tool to empower disadvantaged young people and engage private and public partners to create social change. The idea started in 1996 when Jürgen Griesbeck created "Football for Peace," an initiative that used soccer to combat violence and drugs on the streets of Medellin, Colombia. In 2002, resulting from a global study on Development through Football, which was conducted in cooperation with the International Council for Sports Science and Physical Education, streetfootballworld.org was founded, launching with it a network in Germany.

By 2005, streetfootballworld had spread around the world. Today there are more than 100 organizations using football to beat homelessness and bring peace. India, Peru, United States, South Africa, Kenya, Mali, Rwanda, the UK, Palestinian Authority, Ghana, South Africa, Uganda, Zambia, Brazil, Portugal, Paraguay, Botswana, Burkina Faso, Argentina, and México are some of the countries that have organizations sponsoring street soccer as a way to empower disadvantaged young people around the world. It all started with Jürgen Griesbeck, who created the possibility of peace through empowering youth.[3]

Along similar lines, Mel Young from Scotland and Harald Schmied from Austria created the Homeless World Cup tournament as a way to change the lives of homeless people through football. They held the first Homeless World Cup tournament in Graz, Austria, in 2003. Today, the Homeless World Cup organization coordinates the work of 73 national partners.[4]

*   *   *

Now you. Think about something you are willing to fight for and write it down:

I am willing to fight for _____

_____

_____

_____

---

[3] Reference www.streetfootballworld.org
[4] Reference www.homelessworldcup.org

WRITE YOUR OWN POSSIBILITY STATEMENT

Now that you have practiced a little, I am going to ask you to sit down, meditate, and write your own statement of possibility. This statement declares the world, your environment, your workplace, your school, and your family as ideal. It makes you feel good and it inspires you.

Remember to write your statement in positive terms and in the present tense, narrated as if it already *is*.

For example:

I see the possibility that every customer leaves with a smile.

I see the possibility of kids learning through active exploration.

I see the possibility of a safe environment for whales.

I see the possibility of visually impaired people getting employed.

I see the possibility of the elderly living comfortable, rewarding lives.

I see the possibility that entrepreneurs in retirement help and guide new entrepreneurs.

I see the possibility of a fabulous football field.

I see the possibility of flex-hours at work.

I see the possibility of an incredible personal relationship amongst parents in my school.

You can write whatever inspires you.

Give it a try: *I see the possibility of* _____

_____

_____

_____

Now, you are going to paint an image of the ideal world that is happening or will happen when you live in possibility.

Take a moment and imagine that you are living possibility: what does it look like? What does it feel like? What are people doing? What are *you* doing?

Take your time. Add as much detail as you can. And remember to narrate it in present tense—as if it already is. This will bring a lot of clarity to your mind and will prepare you for the next step.

_____

_____

_____

_____

Now that you have a statement of possibility, try it out. Say it out loud. See how it feels. Does it inspire you? Does it immediately bring up images of what it looks like? Does it spark ideas of things that you could do to make it happen?

When you have written down a statement that you like, share it with others. Listen to yourself as you are saying it. Fine-tune it if you like. And engage others in this conversation.

When you have found a possibility that moves you, and you are able to imagine it clearly, you are ready to go on to Step 2.

STEP 2:
DECLARE AN EVENT,
A PROGRAM,
OR AN INITIATIVE

*It is through conversation and action that you live in possibility
and make possibility happen. – Sergio Sedas*

Now that you have a possibility statement that moves you, it is time to come up with one specific project that manifests this possibility. This project could be an event, a program, or an initiative, but it must impact between 50 and 200 people.

Repeat your statement of possibility out loud and make a list of all the projects, initiatives, and events you can think of that are inspired by this possibility. Do not worry whether you have the resources, the time, or the money to get it done. If it is a project that lives in your possibility, write it down.

*   *   *

Inspired by the possibility of helping a dozen children with cancer, my daughter and two of her friends decided to organize a fundraiser. They contacted a local museum which agreed to host it; renowned artists who agreed to draw paintings which highlighted the outstanding attributes of each child; and newspapers that helped promote the fundraiser.

Many people came, including the mayor, entrepreneurs, and philanthropists. They auctioned off the 12 paintings, and in one night raised over $40,000 to be given to Child AntiCancer Alliance, a nonprofit association that helps children with cancer.

*   *   *

Raised in a small town where the economy had taken a downturn, Martin Martinez, a first-year undergraduate student, created the possibility of new jobs through technology. He went to his hometown, spoke to the mayor, and enrolled him in the possibility of teaching people to program computers so they could hire themselves out to software development companies. Within a few weeks, he had a classroom and 60 people who wanted to learn these new skills. He personally conducted the class.

* * *

In another part of the country, three college students walked by a public hospital and noticed that there were many people camped outside. Inquiring about this, they came to learn that these people had traveled long distances just to bring their loved ones to this hospital. They had been there for a while and did not have the resources to pay for a hotel room or even enjoy a hot lunch.

With this new state of awareness, they decided to do something about it. They launched a fundraiser and invited people to volunteer. With the money they raised, they bought food and took warm lunches to the people camped outside the hospital. This initiative, which started out as a school project, has attracted over 50 volunteers who continue to raise funds to care for and feed the people in need.

Projects that you may want to consider include, but certainly are not limited to:

- A fundraiser for a non-profit organization of your choice
- An event that generates awareness for a cause
- Visiting the elderly in a retirement home
- Planting trees in your community
- A community potluck dinner
- An employment fair
- Networking nights
- After-school activities
- A health drive.

Make your own list. The sky is the limit!

PICK ONE

I hope that you came up with many ideas and that you can identify at least one which you are truly passionate about. For the purpose of this training, I want you to pick only one.

NAME YOUR PROJECT

Give your project a name that people can identify with, become a part of, and talk about. It really does not matter what you call it, but I recommend that the name you choose be simple, short, and catchy. For example:

Toastmasters® — Toastmasters is an international group that attracts professional and non-professional speakers who want to improve and develop great speaking skills.

TED — TED is a series of conferences that capture ideas worth sharing. TED conferences are recorded and shared for free on the Internet.

NOLIMITS —NOLIMITS is the program we developed a number of years ago to help first-year undergraduate mechatronic students learn by doing—building interesting robotic and other mechatronic devices.

Coursera — Coursera is an online platform where universities can share some of their courses. Coursera's reach and influence has grown tremendously in the last five years. It includes free courses from MIT, Carnegie Mellon, Tecnológico de Monterrey, and other top universities around the globe.

Start a list of potential names for your project here: _____

_____

_____

_____

_____

_____

DESCRIBE YOUR PROJECT

Write one or two paragraphs that *clearly* describe the outcome of your project. Imagine that you already completed your project and describe it as it is. Write it in present tense and include as much detail as you can.

When both the purpose and the outcome of a project are clear, people can take initiative and find ways to move your project forward. In contrast, when either the purpose or the outcome is unclear, people hesitate and may get confused. After a while, they lose focus and begin to divert their attention to other things.

SHARE YOUR PROJECT

When you talk to people, remember to state the *possibility* first. Then, follow up with a clear and short description of your project and what you will accomplish. Always describe it in the present tense, as something that already exists, instead of something you plan to do—this will help them visualize it. When everyone on the team is clear about the possibility and the project, they become creative; they generate ideas and alternatives that can help you move your project forward at a faster pace.

NOW IT'S YOUR TURN

Write a clear statement of your project. Make it clear so people understand *what* it is, *when* it is, and *why* it is. Describe it in as much detail as you can.

Write it in the present tense. People can easily imagine things that are expressed in the present tense. They have difficulty imagining things that are declared as things to come.

Let's get to it:

Name your project: _____

Now, write down a statement of your project. Make it clear so people understand what it is, when it is, and why it is. Describe it with as much detail as you can. Describe it in the present as if it already is, not as something that will be. (For example: on every street and in every building, there is ramp access which allows the elderly and physically challenged to enjoy the wonders and benefits our city has to offer.)

_____

_____

_____

_____

_____

_____

_____

_____

_____

By defining the possibility and clearly describing your project, you have established a direction. Now you will move on the next step where you will create your project plan.

NOTES:

STEP 3:
LAY OUT A PLAN

*"Possibility sets the direction; a plan is a map of the road
you will take."* – Sergio Sedas

Have you ever:

*Gone home to relax after a long day at work, only to realize that you forgot to
stop for milk?*

*Jumped into your car to go to an early meeting with only five minutes to spare
and realize you are almost out of gas?*

*Sat down to write that important report due tomorrow, only to realize that
you are out of ink... and it is past midnight?*

*Hosted a party only to realize that you got food but forgot drinks...and the
guests have all arrived?*

While all of these situations are common, they generate unnecessary stress in
your life—and they all could have been prevented with proper planning. With a
plan, you identify what is needed long before it is needed and find solutions to
problems long before they occur.

A detailed plan will give you a roadmap of all the decisions, tasks, time, people,
and resources you need to complete a project. It will help you reduce stress and
give you freedom and the power to prevent failure.

A good and detailed plan will also help you communicate, delegate, and manage
effectively, and keep track of your project. It will help you organize your time
and communicate better to participants, and it will allow you to delegate some

tasks and make better use of your time and your skills. With a good plan, you can focus, get into action, and achieve outstanding results.

PREPARE TO WRITE YOUR PLAN

Once you have a clear idea of your possibility and the project you are going to take on, you are ready to write your plan:

1. Be clear about what you want.

2. Make a general list of everything that has to be in place to complete your project (also called targets).

3. Make a list of the decisions, tasks, time, people, and resources you need to accomplish each target.

4. Assign the people and resources you need to your plan.

BE CLEAR ABOUT WHAT YOU WANT

The first step to create a successful plan is to have a very clear idea of why you are doing this (your purpose and possibility), what you want to accomplish, and what the end result will look like when it is done. The clearer your thoughts are the easier it will be to plan all of the activities, people, and resources needed to get it done.

For example, "*I am having a concert on Friday*" is not as clear as:

> *I am holding a concert on Friday to create awareness for children's cancer. We want to support the efforts of hospitals that are working hard in the fight against cancer in children. I am inviting five local groups and a well-known local singer. We will be hosting it at the school gym that can hold about 500 people. There is space in the immediate parking lot for roughly 100 cars, so we will have shuttles to move people back and forth from a bigger parking lot.*

> *We will sell tickets—between $10 and $15—invite sponsors, and sell snacks and memorabilia during the event. Our Mega Kind Supermarket will donate most of the snacks and beverages. We are inviting all of our friends, people*

from local churches, schools, and the local university as well as people from the Rotary and the company I work for.

Give it a try. Take your time to describe your purpose in full detail, what you want to accomplish, and what the event will look like when it is done. Write down as much detail as you can. Use more paper if you need to. Remember to think about *what* you want to accomplish, and do not worry yet about *how* you are going to do it.

_____

_____

_____

_____

_____

_____

_____

_____

_____

_____

_____

_____

_____

_____

_____

CREATE YOUR PLAN

Now that you have a clear idea of what you are doing and what you wish to accomplish, you need to make a list of everything you will have to put in place to complete your project. You can start with general things that you will call targets. Then, for each target you will make a list of all of the things you must do, decide, ask for, and acquire in order to get it done.

For example, if you were organizing a fundraiser to sponsor a cancer patient operation, you may want to:

- Clearly define the goals and deliverables. For example "Hold an auction to raise $20,000 to donate to Cancer Patients of America."
- Write down a list of things that you must have in place to make this happen. These become your targets. For example:
  o   Get Venue
  o   Raise Sponsorship to Cover Expenses
  o   Make Posters
  o   Invite People
  o   Catering
  o   Get Paintings to the Auction
  o   Publicity
  o   On-Site Hosting of Event

For each of these targets, make a list of specific actions that will help you reach your targets. These actions can include many things including: make a call, make a decision, ask someone for something, make something, draw, post, send an email, pick up, deliver, etc. For example, specific actions for some of your targets could be:

- Make a list of possible venues
- Secure a venue
- Decide on number of guests
- Decide dates
- Get vendor quotes for needed services and supplies
- Ask vendors if they will do it pro-bono

- Make a list of expenses—include venue, catering, publicity, ads, marketing, newspaper, transportation, sound and lights, etc.
- Make a list of possible sponsors
- Contact all sponsors to set up a meeting
- Raise sponsorship to cover expenses
- Open bank account
- Assign treasurer or person responsible for funds
- Request funds
- Follow up until funds are obtained
- Decide on theme
- Bid your project
- Select graphic designers
- Have graphic designer design posters and ad materials
- Get printing quotes
- Select a printer
- Get funds for the printer
- Print posters and ads
- Pick up posters
- Distribute and post posters
- And so on and so forth.
- *Delegate.* Once you build up your team, you want to assign these tasks to members on your team. This will free up your time to update and monitor your project, help and encourage your team, and prevent potential problems from becoming big issues.

Start here with some notes about important tasks you know you'll need to make your possibility move forward.

_____

_____

_____

_____

_____

ASSIGN RESOURCES

Assign the people, money, and other resources that you need to get each task done. In planning, you may come to realize that you need to enroll volunteers and collaborators into your project to take over each of the tasks. You may also discover that you need to ask for money and resources to complete your tasks.

Do you have people in mind for some of your tasks? Put down some thoughts here: _____

_____

_____

NOW IT'S YOUR TURN

On a clean sheet of paper:

- Write down the name of your project.
- Write down a couple of paragraphs which give a clear description of your project. (Remember to look into the future and describe it as it will be once it is completed. Narrate it in the present tense as if it were already successfully completed. And remember to paint a complete picture with juicy details and specific outcomes.)
- Make a master task list of your targets—things that must be in place for your project to happen.
- Under each target, make a list of actions that will accomplish each target.
- For each action, see if you can assign it to a volunteer or a direct member of your team.
- During execution, you want to continuously monitor and update your plan. Mark as *Complete* any task that has been completed. *Add* more tasks as needed. *Remove* tasks that are no longer needed. And *identify critical tasks* that you need to pay special attention to.

TOOLS FOR DRAFTING YOUR PLAN

There are a number of tools that you can use to draft your plan. If it is a small project or if you are just starting out, a simple checklist written on a notepad or in Excel may work. If it is something large and/or complex, you may want to use *mindmaps*, which are great to construct and keep an eye on your project. *Mindjet.com*, *mindmeister.com*, and *mindomo.com* offer great online software to create and update your *mindmaps*.

If you really want to be professional, monitor and manage your project, keep track of your progress, and effectively assign people and resources to each task, you may want to learn to create Gantt charts and use more sophisticated project planners such as Microsoft Project, Zoho Project, and others.

On my web site, www.IntentionalPossibility.com, I have a members' area where you can find worksheets, videos, links, examples, and other resources that will help you become proficient at defining possibility, creating projects, and making them happen.

I have added a list of books, examples, and templates which can help you plan events, meetings, projects, even buildings, among other things, plus a discussion forum where you can share your successes and ask for help.

Be sure to register on the site. Use the Discount Code "IPF" to receive a six-month free subscription as my way of saying, "Thank you for being here and making this world a better place."

NOTES:

STEP 4:
GET INTO ACTION

"Ready, Fire, Aim."
— Jack Canfield[5]

You may have the best plan in the world laid out. You may have all the resources in the world at your disposal. You may have all the time in the world. But unless you take action, nothing ... I repeat, *nothing* ... will happen. Action is what causes things to occur.

History is filled with stories of people who wanted to meet a special someone and—because they did not take the leap—missed out on the love of their life. It is full of stories about people with incredible ideas but never took the step to share them with others or ask for the help they needed to get them done, so they never came to fruition. It is full of wonderful, intelligent people who deserved wealth, love, and joy and yet they never decided to take the first step to get it ... so they didn't get it.

A sale begins with the sales call. Obtaining a college degree starts with filling out an application. Getting a job starts with a resume. And your project begins with one task. Everything in the world—whether it's tangible or not—exists because someone took action.

JUST DO IT

Many people spend their lives planning and waiting until they have generated the "perfect plan." The problem is that if you do this, you never get into action, and therefore nothing gets done.

---

[5] *The Success Principles*, Jack Canfield

The trick to get out of this rut is simply to start. Or, as Nike would say, "Just do it."

In my seminars, I help people start. And once they start, they easily gain momentum.

I ask people to write a breakthrough goal, something that will *really* change their life. Some people think about taking a new position in their company, taking a first-class trip with the family to Europe, starting their own business, studying at a leading university, or writing a book. I encourage them to look for something truly life-changing.

Next, I ask them to make a list of tasks they must do to accomplish this. Do they need to raise funds? Do they need to ask someone for help? Do they need to find out the cost? Do they need to research travel options and book a flight? You get the picture.

Finally, I ask them to think about one thing they could do *in 15 minutes* that could move their project forward. I give them a few minutes to decide. Then, I ask them to stand up and *do it*.

Until you do this exercise, you cannot imagine how simple it is to move your project forward. Yet once you take action, you continue to do so until you gain momentum. What I have experienced is that by taking the first step, the breakthrough goal that everyone sees as out of reach quickly becomes real.

*   *   *

When I first heard of this exercise, I was participating in a seminar led by Jack Canfield. He asked us to declare a breakthrough goal. I declared, "Having a wonderful and romantic life with my wife."

Next, he asked us to determine one thing we could do in 15 minutes to move our goal forward. I remembered that, in a few days, I would be meeting my wife in Vegas (something we had wanted to do for some time now). I wrote down that I would call the hotel and ask them to deliver a wonderful bouquet of white roses to our room, so when my wife saw them she would know how much I love her. I chose white, because they are her favorites, and they have significance in our life and relationship. So, I found the number for the hotel, asked them for a bouquet of white roses, told them what to write on the card, gave my credit card number, and returned to the seminar room. All of this in less than 15 minutes.

A couple days later, my wife and I met at the hotel in Vegas and checked in. My experience was incredible. Ever since I made the phone call a few days earlier, I filled myself with excitement and anticipation of what it would be like when she opened the door to our room and saw the incredible bouquet of white roses ordered specially for her.

We walked into our room … and there they were. In front of us was the most amazing bouquet of white roses I have ever seen. The roses were huge and incredibly beautiful. An image of perfection you can only find in a place that honors elegance and a wonderful experience. Needless to say, my wife was incredibly moved and excited to see them. In one instant she realized the amazing woman that she is and how significant she is in my life. That set the tone for an incredibly romantic weekend for both of us.

Fifteen minutes is all it took—15 minutes.

*   *   *

This principle can be used in any area of life, personal or professional.

Here is another example:

Ismael Muñoz is the founder of Fitness Academy in México, a very successful health and fitness program that has inspired and helped many people defeat obesity and become healthy and slim[6]. Fitness Academy was born out of the possibility of helping people recover their health and feel sure and confident about themselves.

When I first started working with Ismael, before he started Fitness Academy, I asked him two very simple questions: think of a project you can do that will influence between 50 and 200 people; and think of one thing you can do in the next 15 minutes to move your project forward.

---

[6] Fitness Academy http://www.fitnessacademy.mx/

A year later, he has a successful business that is running a highly-motivational, custom-designed, twelve-week program that takes participants into increased health and fitness.

Fifteen minutes is all it took.

*   *   *

WHAT CAN YOU DO IN 15 MINUTES?

Make a list of the things you could do to move your project forward. Pick one that you can do in just 15 minutes:

- Make a phone call to gather needed information.
- Call your friend to ask for a person's phone number.
- Send an email.
- Schedule a meeting.
- Write one page for your new book.
- Discuss your idea with someone.
- Start on an assignment that you have been putting off.
- Schedule a meeting with your coach.
- Acknowledge someone.
- Ask someone for a whiteboard you can use.

There are so many things that could be done in 15 minutes to start you on your path to cause an amazing change in your life, your income, your romance, and your happiness.

Write down some things right now that you can do in 15 minutes:

_____

_____

_____

_____

Now stop reading. Get up from your seat. *Do it.*

PERFECT IS GOOD. DONE IS BETTER!

One thing that holds us back from moving forward is the thought of perfection. Is my plan perfect? Will I succeed? What if something goes wrong? What if it fails?

Does all action produce immediate favorable results? No.

Does all action take us where we expect? No.

Can we predict everything? No!

Regardless of how uncomfortable or uncertain you feel about the outcome, take the first step and run with your plan. And be open to the fact that your plan may change and that the outcome may be different than what you expected. Things are unpredictable, and that is OK. Take action and adjust along the way.

Perfect is good. Done is better!

Jack Canfield once taught me the phrase: *"Ready? FIRE! Aim."* It is not until you *fire* that you can see if you hit the target. And if you did not hit the target, you simply make the necessary corrections and try again. Do this a sufficient number of times and YOU WILL HIT YOUR TARGET!

Perfect is good. Done is better!

NOTES: _____

STEP 5:
ENGAGE OTHERS

" Manage people and they will get tasks done;
lead them and they will jump into action;
engage them in possibility and they will change the
world." — Sergio Sedas

Now that you have a clear idea of what you are going to do, it is time for you to enlist people into your project. You want people to keep you motivated and to help you organize, lead, manage, communicate, raise funds, deliver, pick up, write, call, receive, and perform the dozens of tasks that need to get done.

You will need people to give you resources, money, equipment, and transportation. You will also need people to share the project with others and get the community excited about it; experts to manage the funds and set up communications, websites and media; and people with leadership and administrative skills that can manage and lead your team.

Volunteers make up some of the best members on your team. Once they are engaged in possibility, they become highly motivated and committed to the project. At that point, they are emotionally driven to willingly give their time, resources, and experience to help others.

Did you know that over 1.1 million volunteers responded to the aftermath of Hurricane Katrina, providing more than 14 million hours of service to people in need?

Or that over 500 volunteers joined together in Boston to renovate homes and non-profit facilities on National Rebuilding Day?

Volunteers are responsible for hundreds, if not thousands, of things that enrich our lives. They help organize the company picnic, or a mothers' night out, or a day to read stories in elders' homes. They pick up the garbage in empty lots, build a park, teach reading in adult night classes, raise funds to fix a clock in the town square, launch a photo contest, organize a conference, and teach kids about the beauties of the world.

Whether you engage one, two, or a hundred volunteers into your possibility, you want to start today.

ENGAGE THEM INTO POSSIBILITY

In my experience, engaging people into possibility happens in three steps:

1. Share the possibility with passion.

2. Listen carefully.

3. Ask for what you need and want.

SHARE THE POSSIBILITY WITH PASSION

People will join you and your project when they are excited about it, they resonate with it, and they clearly see how and what they can contribute. Share your possibility with everyone in such a way that they are inspired and become engaged and motivated.

How do you do this? By being excited and authentic and talking about possibility from the heart.

Get fired up. Go to people and share what is possible. Paint a clear picture and create an emotional connection. Articulate a vision so bright, so magnificent, that they feel they have to come along for the ride. You will soon realize that people respond well when they know their work is contributing to a great cause that is bigger than themselves. Communicate that vision.

LISTEN CAREFULLY

Once you communicate the vision, stop for a moment and *LISTEN* to what people have to say when you are sharing with them. Really listen and be genuinely interested in what they tell you. Ask them questions. Listen carefully to their ideas. And find out what resonates with them, what they are good at, and what they like to do.

They will soon begin to offer suggestions, give you ideas, and tell you what you should do. Listen to them. Thank them. They are engaged.

ASK FOR WHAT YOU NEED AND WANT

People can help you in many ways. They can help you come up with ideas for your project. They can serve as your council or your idea bouncing-board. They can help you with money, ideas, venues, and time. They can be leaders. They can be hosts. They can design. They can post.

They can pick somebody up from the airport. They can arrange transportation. They can make a call. They can do the bookkeeping. They can raise funds. They can put up posters—and they can take them down. They can involve others. They can cheer you on. People can help you in so many ways.

And they *will* help you. But there is one thing you must do: *you must **ask**.*

- *Ask* for what you need;
- *Ask* for what you want;
- *Ask* them to join you;
- *Ask* them for ideas;
- *Ask* them for connections;
- *Ask* them for help.

Without hesitation and with a lot of gratitude, simply go to them and *ask*.

HOW TO ENGAGE PARTICIPANTS

1. Make a list of people and organizations you would like to invite into your project.

2. Share the possibility and the project with them. Listen to their thoughts and ideas, and ask them to join you.

3. Make a list of things that you need and want. For example: someone to do your bookkeeping, someone to pick something up, someone to provide funds, someone to enlist sponsors, etc.

4. Go to the people and organizations on your list and *ask*.

Now it's your turn: start now by making your lists and engaging others into your possibility.

STEP 6:
CELEBRATE

Most projects will take weeks, if not months, of preparation. Therefore, it is important to keep everyone focused and motivated throughout. One way to do this is to constantly repeat the statement of possibility and to celebrate and acknowledge each other along the way. Celebration motivates people, relieves tension, and generates the positive energy required to get the job done.

START WITH "WHAT IS NEW AND GOOD"

A common mistake leaders make is to focus solely on what needs to get done, without taking time to acknowledge and appreciate what has been completed. This results in tension among your team. Knowing what needs to get done is important, but so is acknowledging and appreciating the progress you have made. Taking a moment to celebrate that you have completed 30% of the project can be much more stimulating than remembering that you still have 70% to go.

In his book, *Success Principles*, Jack Canfield suggests starting each meeting with a round in which each person of the team is encouraged to take a few minutes to share "what is new and good." Everyone in the team talks about whatever is going on in his or her life and takes the time to celebrate and acknowledge themselves for the things—large or small—that they have done in the last few days.

Just this exercise alone has a great positive impact on the energy level of your team. People who are troubled by something are given a nurturing space to vent it out. And everyone feels good after sharing their positive progress.

After a round of "what is new and good" the team is energized and prepared to seek and overcome new challenges.

SHARE PHOTOS AND JOURNAL ENTRIES

Whether they are participating on your team or not, people will begin to root for you. They are excited about the possibility. They are excited about your project. And they are excited about you.

Keep up their spirits by sharing pictures and journals of your progress. You and your team met a sponsor? Share it! You designed the posters? Share them! Your guest speaker has said 'yes'? SHARE IT!

People are inspired by what you are doing. And they are living your project through you.

Document it and SHARE IT!

AFTER YOUR PROJECT IS OVER ... CELEBRATE!

The day will come when you have finally completed the project. You are done, and everyone did a great job. Now it is time to truly celebrate. Congratulate the team. Thank your sponsors. And thank your fans.

Organize a party. Have music. Make noise. Share the pictures. Make it memorable, and make it fun.

During the party, or in the next few days, take the time to personally acknowledge your team and everyone who contributed to make the possibility happen.

Every one of us wants to feel significant and appreciated. In that context, it is a wonderful feeling to know that who we are and what we have done has greatly contributed to the happiness and well being of others. Ask yourself:

1.   What are some of the ways you can celebrate with your team?

2.   What are some things you can do to acknowledge members of your team and collaborators?

3. What are some of the ways you can celebrate and share your progress with the community?

It's your turn now—think of ways to celebrate your team and their accomplishments, and do it!

Think of some ways you can celebrate with your team and share your accomplishments:

_____

_____

_____

_____

_____

_____

_____

_____

_____

_____

_____

NOTES:

SHOWSTOPPERS

I was just about to dial when I began to have second thoughts:
What if they do not approve?
What will others think?
What if I lose my job?

As you venture into your project, you may fall into one of the five most common roadblocks that may attempt to hold you back:

- lack of clarity
- resistance
- ego
- expectations
- fear.

Resistance, ego, expectations, and fear live inside of you in the form of thoughts, and they can awaken any time you decide to pursue something different. They make you feel uncomfortable. They make you feel defeated. They make you worry. They work in unison in an intense plot to make you turn back, pull you out of your path, and make you forget the possibility that you created.

But don't worry—you are not alone, and there are ways to defeat these roadblocks:

To defeat lack of clarity—gain clarity and define clearly.

To defeat resistance—get into action, prepare, face the fear.

To defeat ego—let go of the ego; get into action.

To defeat expectations—let go of the expectations.

To defeat fear—feel the fear and move forward anyway.

If you find yourself challenged by any of these roadblocks, details about how each of these might manifest itself in your project plus exercises for you to complete to overcome them will be available soon on our website. Bookmark www.IntentionalPossibility.com to be the first to learn of new materials.

When you overcome one or more roadblocks as you pursue your passion and possibility, you will see and savor the immensity of what you are able to create—and that will give you the confidence you need to break through other roadblocks as they rise up along your way.

GO 'PRO'

Congratulations! You stuck it out, and you have really come a long way. You invented an inspiring and passionate possibility. Within possibility, you defined a project that influenced between 50 and 200 people. You laid out a plan, formed a team, and began to execute it. Along the way, you inspired others and brought out the leader within you. Take a moment to sit down, look back, and enjoy this moment.

Now on to the final step. You are going to work on six key elements that will take you and your leadership to the next level. These are:

1. **Maintain your drive:** *People do not follow ideas, they follow passion. Learn to live and communicate with passion, and people will follow.*
2. **Become the master of focus:** *Learn to do the right things, quickly and efficiently; focus and become effective in everything you do … and you will accomplish the extraordinary.*
3. **Master integrity:** *Define and declare your principles and values, then live them.*
4. **Communicate with passion and meaning:** *When you are a pro, communication takes on a new dimension—you're playing in the big leagues and need to connect, convey, and deliver.*
5. **Be outrageous:** *Becoming a pro means doing whatever it takes to accomplish your goal—even things you would normally consider 'outrageous.'*
6. **Ask, Ask, Ask:** *When you take a big leap into your possibility, you will find that you need to reach out and ask for help, resources, money, and time.*

More information about these key elements to 'going pro' as well as detailed exercises to help you become comfortable and proficient with them will be available soon—bookmark www.IntentionalPossibility.com to be the first to learn of new materials.

I discovered that the only way to learn to live possibility and make great things happen is ... to live possibility and work to make a great project happen—to do something that excites you and at the same time, pushes you way out of your comfort zone.

IT'S NOT ABOUT THE PROCESS—IT'S ABOUT YOU

You are about to immerse yourself fully into your project and live one of the most exciting, strongest, and most life-altering experiences of your life. As you live this process, I want you to keep this in mind:

The process is NOT about the project, but about YOU living the process.

You see, in the process of making the project happen, you will face challenges that you must overcome and situations that move you far out of your comfort zone. As you face and overcome those challenges, you will increase your self-confidence and develop the skills you will use to launch new initiatives, structure a plan, and enroll and lead others to make them happen.

I want you to live the process of generating possibility, force yourself into facing challenges and situations that will help you increase your self-confidence, and master skills along the way.

The game is on. *The only rule is to play the game full-out!*

BRING PROSPERITY INTO YOUR LIFE

Bringing prosperity into your life is a combination of two things: having a clear idea of what a life of prosperity means to you, and generating the mindset, time, and money to do it. Both exist in possibility.

In my next book, *Intentional Possibility in Action: your way into prosperity*, we will work together to help create the mindset, the time, and the money you need to live your life fully in possibility. You will become clear about what moves you and declare a life of prosperity in every aspect of your life—your finances, your travel and entertainment, your family, your social contributions, your work, and your health.

You will jump into the possibility and make it happen. You will define your ideal job, plan your next trip, start a company, or flourish in your organization. You will define your intentions and goals. You will brainstorm and generate creative ways to get there, leveraging who you are. You will lay out a meaningful plan and enroll others.

You will take action with commitment, passion, and focus, which will lead you into generating the momentum you need to move forward. You will ask for what you need and eagerly learn what you need to learn.

You will overcome resistance, expectations, and fear. You will monitor your progress and use this knowledge to correct your thoughts and actions along your path. And you will acknowledge and celebrate every single step of the way.

Intentional Possibility = your way into prosperity

YOUR NEW BEGINNING

I am very excited!

You are ready to play the game. You are ready to put into motion your own possibility with actions that will change the lives of people around you. You, too, will experience change and the wonderful feeling of significance that comes from giving unconditionally and seeing your dreams and projects come true.

You started by understanding possibility and how you can intentionally tap into possibility to create a wonderful life for those around you. You are now ready to create a project that involves and influences between 50 and 200 people.

By living the process, you will learn how to enroll people into your project and how to create a network of friends, colleagues, and volunteers to make it happen. You will learn to plan and set clear goals and objectives. You will learn to delegate and you will learn to ask. You will learn the way.

Every day you will be faced with the challenges that occur when one dares to go beyond their comfort zone to create something great. And you will learn how to face those challenges with integrity, commitment, and diligence.

Continue to live in possibility. This is your new beginning!

TESTIMONIALS FOR INTENTIONAL POSSIBILITIES

How would you feel if you were surrounded by people who were excited, willing to work together and help each other out, eager to face new challenges and adversities, passionate, and driven by a positive sense of purpose and contribution to others? What if these were your kids? What if these were your colleagues? What if this was YOU?

A couple of years ago, we launched a program to help young adults increase resiliency, intrinsic motivation and self-confidence, and help them find their sense of purpose. The program is a live workshop experience that teaches Jack Canfield's *Success Principles™* and our own *Intentional Possibility*.

In this program, students just like you take on the *Intentional Possibility Challenge*. They declare possibility, create a project that has a positive impact for 50 to 200 people, and enroll volunteers. Through the process they experience tremendous personal growth.

We consistently found that people who participate full-out in the process live a transformational experience. They build a network that gives them confidence and support. They gain a sense of significance and a strong sense of purpose. They learn to ask for what they need. They face and overcome challenges and adversities and realize that they have what it takes to overcome them.

They become great leaders. They learn that they can find people who are willing and able to help them. They learn to inspire and enroll people into their possibility and to create a community that works together to make it happen. They learn responsibility and how to do things outside their comfort zone because they are moved by responsibility and commitment to a greater good.

In a very short time frame, they experience tremendous growth and develop the skills, the positive attitude, and the mindset we desire in our leaders and people who work in our organizations.

But perhaps I should let some of our graduates share their experiences in their own words:

"This program has given me great personal growth. It showed me the importance of knowing yourself, of accepting yourself, and, above all, appreciating yourself so you can be a light of inspiration for others. Every day you wake up wanting to fulfill a purpose that is your LIFE PURPOSE and to take actions that become your goals.

"Why not start today? Give yourself the opportunity and joy that comes through motivating yourself and others, appreciating, valuing yourself, and feeling that you deserve this opportunity that God and life give you. I give thanks to Sergio Sedas for teaching us and, above all, for the passion and love with which he has shared this program."

- María Fernanda Molina Pereira- Barranquilla, Colombia

"I was able to be myself; I learned to see what I wanted; and I learned that I can meet my goals. [This program] taught me how to do it and how to continue doing it. How to overcome challenges and difficult times, etc. I recommend it because what I learned is amazing and what I take with me is to believe in myself. I am in high frequency."

– Manuel Medina , Monterrey Nuevo Leon

"Great job! Dr. Sedas knows what he is doing, he has a lot of experience, but most of all, he knows how to teach it and express it in an extraordinary way. I was able to write and visualize my goals and I highly recommend this program because it changes your way to see life and everything around you."

- Mauricio Galindo Monterrey

"[The program] completely changed my life and the way I see things in my life. I now face everything with a positive attitude and daily I grow and become a better person."

- Juan Martín Martínez Reyna, San Buenaventura, Coahuila

"I was able to look inside of myself and realize what I am made of. A great experience full of different things every day. I left the workshop feeling more complete, more focused and determined to live my life purpose, and to appreciate the people I love. In search of a rich life full of immeasurable experiences."

- R. Polendo Monterrey

"I recommend [this program] because it changes your perspective of life. I recommend it because since I took the program I wake up more positive, with courage and willingness to continue and face problems that cross my path."

- María Paulina Durán Lerma, Monterrey

"I recommend it a lot because you become aware of so many things that you did not know before. Teamwork is excellent. Having goals. Acknowledging your own successes is something we seldom do yet is so good for us."

- Marcelo del Bosque, Monterrey

"I was able to draft my life plan, which can improve in time to adapt itself to the vision I have for myself."

- Víctor Manuel Gómez González, Monterrey, N.L.

"I learned to know myself. Sincerely I believe it to be one of the best programs I have been in, I feel very motivated. I realized that I am a person with many dreams and aspirations and now I have intentionally awakened new possibilities. Furthermore, I have found a way to transcend in life. I have realized that I am a person who can cause positive change in other people's lives. I now know who I am, what I like, where I am going and who I love in my life. Thank you for helping me become a person who appreciates life, what I have and what is to come."

- Luis Gallardo, Monterrey

"Intentional Possibility is a way to give meaning to your goals and your leadership."

- Elías Perry Cárdenas

"To be unreasonable in my passions is something that has allowed me to be where I am today. I had never thought about this, and from now on, I will continue to be' unreasonable' even more."

- José Gutiérrez

THE
INTENTIONAL POSSIBILITY
CHALLENGE

In different places around the world, people like you have chosen to take the **INTENTIONAL POSSIBILITY** Challenge. Through this challenge they have declared possibility and started initiatives that have touched the lives of thousands of people in their communities, their organizations, and their workplaces.

You can, too!

TAKE THE INTENTIONAL POSSIBILITY CHALLENGE!

✓ Declare possibility.

✓ Take on a project that impacts the lives of 50 to 200 people.

✓ Enroll at least 20 volunteers to help you create it, be part of it, and give it life.

✓ Then share your story.

Join us at www. INTENTIONALPOSSIBILITY.com

TAKE
INTENTIONAL POSSIBILITY
TO YOUR SCHOOL, COMPANY, AND ORGANIZATION

Take the **INTENTIONAL POSSIBILITY** Program into your school, company and/or organization. Help your team develop the passion, drive, and confidence to take on new challenges, overcome adversity, and move with purpose and passion. Lead them in a process through which they will learn to launch new initiatives and inspire people to join them.

Ask about our Conferences, In-house Programs, and Train-the-Trainer Programs.

Find out more at
www.INTENTIONALPOSSIBILITY.com

DO YOU NEED MORE COPIES OF

INTENTIONAL POSSIBILITY

TO SHARE WITH YOUR COLLEAGUES, FAMILY, ORGANIZATION, OR COMMUNITY?

Once you discover the power of possibility, you will want to share it with your family and friends, your co-workers, and your community. Discounts are available for orders of 25 or more copies. Custom editions can be made for your group with an order of 100 or more copies. *Declare and share possibility now!*

For more information
visit www. INTENTIONALPOSSIBILITY.com

WOULD YOU LIKE TO HAVE DR. SEDAS
SPEAK TO YOUR GROUP
TO SHARE THE MAGIC AND POWER OF
INTENTIONAL POSSIBILITY?

The magic and power of Intentional Possibility is available to everyone, no matter their location. Dr. Sedas is available to speak to your company, nonprofit, community, or class to guide you through the process that will help you change the world.

For more information
visit www. INTENTIONALPOSSIBILITY.com

NOTES:

NOTES: _____

NOTES:

NOTES:

CPSIA information can be obtained
at www.ICGtesting.com
Printed in the USA
FSHW04n2328160418
47045FS